D1277490

FRESH PICKED
for all Seasons

by Dodi Lee Poulsen of Two Sisters at Squirrel Hollow

Landauer Publishing

FRESH PICKED
for all Seasons

by Dodi Lee Poulsen of Two Sisters at Squirrel Hollow

Copyright© 2010 by Landauer Corporation

Fresh Picked projects
Copyright© 2010 by Dodi Lee Poulsen

This book was designed, produced,
and published by Landauer Books
A division of Landauer Corporation
3100 101st Street, Urbandale, IA 50322
www.landauercorp.com   800/557-2144

President/Publisher: Jeramy Lanigan Landauer
Vice President of Sales and Operations: Kitty Jacobson
Managing Editor: Jeri Simon
Art Director: Laurel Albright
Photographer: Sue Voegtlin

All rights reserved. No part of this book may be reproduced or
transmitted in any form by any means, electronic or mechanical,
including photocopying, recording, or by any information storage
and retrieval system without permission in writing from the
publisher, except as noted. The publisher presents the information
in this book in good faith. No warranty is given, nor are
results guaranteed.

ISBN 13: 978-0-9825586-5-2
ISBN 10:   0-9825586-5-1

Library of Congress Control Number: 2010926608

This book printed on acid-free paper.
Printed in China

10-9-8-7-6-5-4-3-2-1

Dodi Lee Poulsen grew up in Northern California in a close-knit family of two brothers and a sister. Her love of fabric and the art of the needle came honestly and naturally to her. She recalls, *"One of my favorite memories is sitting on my Grandmother's lap when I was about four, helping Nana push fabric through a treadle sewing machine. At ten, with my mother's gentle guidance, I created my first sewn garment, a blouse. It didn't take me long to realize the sewing machine and I would be lifelong partners."*

Dodi's BFA college degree in interior design launched a 25 year career as a free lance interior designer where, in her own company, In the Beginning Creations, she created home decorating projects and devoted many years honing her color and fabric design skills. Quilting has been a passion ever since she created textile projects during college years. For more than 20 years, Dodi has shared her quilting passion, teaching the art of quilting and lecturing to students throughout the country.

In 2006, Dodi and her sister, Heidi began their pattern company, Two Sisters at Squirrel Hollow. Working together in a wonderful quilt studio overlooking the woods on Heidi's 10 acres in Missouri, they have created fresh and youthful patterns that have quickly gained them an enthusiastic following in the quilt market. Dodi's daughter, Megan, has now joined the business as designer for Little Londyn, a children's division of Two Sisters at Squirrel Hollow.

Today, Dodi happily designs and creates quilts at home in the state of Washington as well as during frequent visits to Squirrel Hollow. The beautiful Northwest provides an incredible backdrop for inspiration. Dodi also loves to spend time in her garden where she finds nature creating the best lessons in color and design.

"For me, quilting embraces emotion and beautifully blends fabric with the heart of its creator."

Family life takes center stage for Dodi. She and her husband Bart have raised a son Mikel and a daughter Megan and now have 4 grandchildren. As a new grandmother, she has quickly begun sharing her love of sewing. *"My older grandchildren love to sit on my lap pushing fabric through the sewing machine, just as I did as a child so many years ago."*

Table of Contents

4

Apple Collection 78

Pear Collection 90

Fresh Picked
for all Seasons

There is nothing I love better than feasting on my favorite fruits as they come into season each year. Their vibrant colors and delicious freshness are captivating. I can't wait for each season of goodness to come to market.

Larger scale novelty fabrics featuring the abundance of the harvest were my inspiration for the collections in this book. Each year fabric manufacturers duplicate nature at its best on fabrics. Fabrics have never been more beautiful. Big is in... and the bolder the better!

I adore the whimsical nature of novelty fabrics. The projects in this book are equally geared to other fabrics as well. Combine novelty prints with sassy basics and you'll have fabulous projects.

It's amazing what creative energies are released when you step outside your comfort zone. You can create and add your own personal touch using these fun fabrics for yourself and your home. Not to mention all the lovely gifts you'll be able to make for friends! Adding that special touch has never been easier.

Included in some of the designs are my favorite pre-cut fabrics. Layer cakes, strips and honey buns can be used in several of the designs that make them simple and easy to create in a short amount of time. Even if you are new to sewing, you can make these delightful projects. Create an entire collection in your favorite fabrics!

I hope you'll enjoy the ideas in my book. Have fun with them and add your own personal style by choosing fabrics and trims reflective of your personal tastes. Here's to Fresh Picked goodness!

All My Best,

Dodi

dodipoulsen@twosashquilts.com

www.twosashquilts.com

6

General Instructions

We do our very best to test & proof our patterns, but sometimes an error will slip by us. Before starting any project we recommend you visit our website at www.twosashquilts.com & check under Squirrel Tails. We post pattern corrections there. If you catch an error, please let us know. Thank you!

Please read all instructions before beginning any project.

- Yardages are based on 42" fabrics. Please make allowances if your fabric is narrower.

- Seam allowances are 1/4" unless otherwise noted.

- For best results use 100% cotton fabrics from a quality quilt shop. Cotton fabric minimizes seam distortion, presses well and is easy to quilt on.

- Double check all block measurements by laying your clear ruler over the block to ensure correct size. Don't continue to the next step unless they are correct.

- RST means right sides together.

Seam Allowances

We cannot stress enough the importance of accuracy in seam allowances. Test your machine to confirm your seam width. A 1/4"-foot is a life saver and most machines offer this option.

Pressing Tips

- Pressing is the key to successful piecing & quiltmaking. PRESS, do not iron! Don't move the iron back & forth, simply lift the iron up & down & spritz with a little bit of water if necessary. Don't use steam on blocks. Steam can easily distort your fabrics & make them stretch out of shape.

- Most important, every seam must be pressed before the next is added. This will create accuracy & success!

starch

Ever wonder why your quilt blocks don't turn out just right? The correct preparation of the fabric makes all the difference! Starching quilt fabrics makes cutting, piecing, appliquéing and quilting easier. Starched fabric cuts easily, even when stacked together, and sews together beautifully. It will hold sharp creases, including those made by finger pressing. A block made of starched fabric when pressed during construction will not shrink or become otherwise distorted. It's Extra Work, you say! But It's worth the effort because.....

Starching tames the bias edge. Starch makes all fabrics equal. Homespuns will behave just like batiks, once it is starched. Starched fabric will give you more control as you stitch. Starched quilt fabric doesn't shift as you rotary cut. Appliqués turn easier with a crisper fold. It makes it easy to make perfect appliquéd circles. Quilting is full of opinions & options. Each quilt is different; each quilter, too. To starch or not to starch is up to you.

My personal favorite starch is a Niagara® non-aerosol spray. Or, you can also easily make your own using 50% water and 50% bottled starch for yardage. STARCH fabrics before starting any project and you won't be disappointed.

Two Sisters Tip

When starching, spray fabric on one side, fold the other half of the fabric on top and press. This way the starch will go directly into the fibers of the fabric and not on your iron. Hooray! It is best to starch more than once - several times does the trick! Reverse the fold and continue starching until you get a crisp piece of fabric.

General Instructions

Pinning

We know you hate to pin, but for the best success, take the time to do it. Pinning reduces slipping, stretching & makes your finished product one you can be proud of.

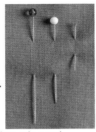

Nesting seams

When smaller pieced units are required to be pieced together to make a larger block the results will be accurate and polished if you nest the seams. The seams should be pressed in opposite directions from each other so the seam allowance falls in alternate sides of the crossing seam line. Place the 2 units RST matching the seam line. Rub your finger on top and you will see they will nest into each other perfectly. Place a pin on each side of the crossing seam line and stitch into place.

setting seams

Before you press a seam allowance to one side, put your iron down on it flat, just as it was sewn. Don't move the iron back and forth; just lift the iron up and down. This step "sets" the seam, encouraging the seam to go in the direction of the side on which it was pressed.

NO FUSS FAST FUSE Machine Appliqué

Many projects in this book use fusible web and are machine appliquéd to cover the raw edges. It is important to have your machine set up for the best possible results. Following the instructions below, set up your machine in the configuration that will best suit your project.

Machine set-up

1. Make certain your machine is clean and in good working order.
2. Install a new size 60/8, 70/10, 75/11, or 80/12 sharp universal or embroidery needle in your machine.
3. Wind a bobbin with cotton 50 or 60-weight embroidery thread or bobbin-fill thread.
4. Thread the needle with matching or complementary color 50 or 60-weight thread.
5. Set your machine for a zigzag stitch with a width between 1 and 1.5mm or about 1/8" wide. Set the stitch length just above (not at) the satin-stitch setting, or between .5 and 1mm.
6. If possible, set your machine in the "needle down" position and set the motor at half speed.

Machine Applique

All pattern pieces are cut without seam allowances. The raw edges are covered with a close machine satin, buttonhole, or decorative stitch.

Using the correct fusible web for your project will be key in its success. Fusible web has an adhesive surface on both sides of the web allowing you to iron it to both the template shape and then onto the fabric.

Currently there are many fusible products to choose from. If you will be hand tracing your deign to the fusible web Lite Steam a Seam 2® or Shades SoftFuse® are ideal.

If you want this to be a painless process try the new Print N' Fuse® fusible webbing. This allows you to print your templates directly onto your webbing without having to trace, saving you an entire step and providing accurate templates! Using this method makes for a NO FUSS FAST FUSE project. Follow manufacturer's instructions for this product.

General instructions for fusible web

First, starch your fabric two or three times following the method stated above in the Starch section. This provides a crisp piece that has stability while you cut your shapes out.

Trace or print your template onto the paper side of the fusible web. Leave enough room between shapes to loosely cut them out around the printed or traced line. Do not cut on the traced or printed line at this point. If the shape is more than 2" in diameter it is a good idea to cut out the center of the shape leaving an outer ring of approximately 1/4" – 1/2". This allows the fabric to remain soft and pliable making it easier to quilt and embroider.

Iron the selected fusible web pieces, paper side up, onto the wrong side of fabrics following manufacturer's instructions. Let cool. Cut pieces out directly on the traced or printed line.

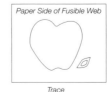

Trace

Position and Fuse   *Cut*

Arrange pieces onto your quilt block, placing background pieces first, and then work forward layering them.

Peel paper off. Following manufacturer's instructions, fuse appliqué to background fabric.

Peel

Right Side of Fabrics

Arrange and Fuse

Use a stabilizer, tissue paper or a commercially made fabric on the back side while appliquéing. Tear off stabilizer after complete. Using a stabilizer will allow your fabric to move smoothly though the machine when appliquéing while providing stability for the fabric.

Two Sisters Tip

I like to use an appliqué pressing sheet. You can lay out and position your appliqué pieces and fuse them together before you fuse them to your project.

Invisible Appliqué

Use an invisible thread on the top of your machine & a standard weight thread in the bobbin. This gives the look of hand appliqué in very little time.

Use an invisible blind hem stitch to attach pattern pieces to background fabric. You may need to adjust the tension on your machine.

Bias strips & Binding

Strips for bias binding are cut on the bias, diagonally across the grain of fabric, which runs at a 45-degree angle against the selvage. When the fabric is cut on the bias it allows for the most stretch.

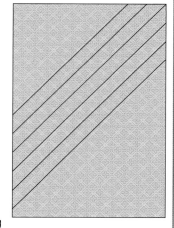

To cut fabric on the bias start with a square or rectangle piece of fabric. Make a cut at a 45-degree angle in the center of the fabric. Cut additional strips out from the center to outer edges utilizing the longer pieces of fabric. (See diagram) Cut strips the desired width parallel to the edge. Cut enough strips to complete the project. The strips will be joined together in the same way as in straight binding.

Bias Binding for Quilt Top

If cutting bias binding for a scalloped or curved edge of a quilt the binding will be a single fold 1" finished piece. Cut the bias strip 1-1/2" wide. Using a 1" bias tape maker, follow manufacturer's instructions to make the tape. Open bias tape on one edge and sew to quilt top. Fold over and hand sew to back side.

Needle sizes

Not all needle sizes are created equal. Stitch quality is affected by the needle and the thread. They go hand in hand and create a successful sewing experience that eliminates skipped stitches, puckered seams, and broken threads. Always start with a fresh, new needle for every sewing project. If stitching problems occur, always change the needle. A dull or burred needle can cause snags and puckering. Select the size of the sewing needle based on the weight of the fabric and the size or type of thread being used.

For general purposes these needles are recommended:

• General Piecing - needle size 80/12

• For machine appliqué – needle size 70/10

• For heavier thread, usually topstitch- needle size 90/14 jeans needle.

It is recommended that you don't use heavy weight thread in your bobbin. You may need to adjust the tension on your machine. When using a heavier weight thread, changing the size of your needle accommodates the thread weight to prevent fraying.

Surefire Matching Technique

When you are joining one unit to another it is helpful to use a positioning pin. With RST, push a pin vertically through the intersection of the seam at the 1/4" seam line. Continue pushing pin through bottom block, lining up the 1/4" seam lines.

Keep this pin standing upright so the fabrics won't shift. To hold the fabrics together as shown, pin on either side of the positioning pin, remove the positioning pin. As you sew, remove each pin as it nears the needle.

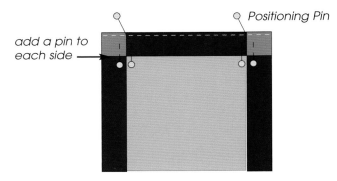

Positioning Pin

add a pin to each side

Borders

- Measure width of quilt top through center, top & bottom. Take an average of this measurement. Cut the two border pieces to this measurement.

- Sew the two borders to the top & bottom of quilt. Repeat this process for the length of quilt. Press seams toward border.

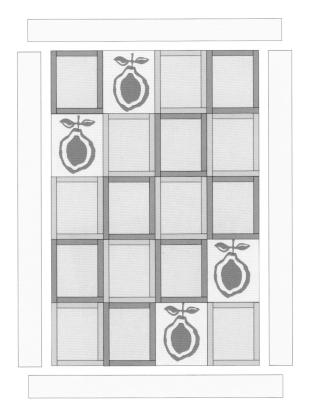

Using Lengthwise of Fabric for Borders

I like to cut borders from the length of the fabric. This eliminates any seams in the border & makes for a nice flat finish with no "waves". Borders can be a beast to manage when they are wavy. If you cut your borders on the length of the grain, or parallel to the selvage edge, you will eliminate most of the problems. You can use the leftover fabric in the backing or put it in your stash.

Mitered Borders

Mitered borders are not cut to the exact measurement. You will miter them and then cut off the remaining fabric at the end of the process.

1. To find center of border fold it in half and mark with a pin. Place border strip and quilt top RST and sew beginning and ending 1/4" from quilt top corners. Allow excess border fabric to extend beyond edges of quilt top. Repeat for remaining border strips. Back-stitch to secure. Press seams toward border.

2. Lay quilt top right side up on ironing board or hard surface. Fold each border end flat back onto itself, right sides together, forming a 45-degree angle at the quilt's corner. Press to form sharp creases.

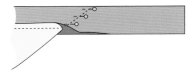

3. Fold quilt on diagonal, right sides together. Align the border strip's raw edges, the border seams at the 1/4" point, and the creases; pin in place. Stitch along crease, backstitching at 1/4" border seam.

4. With quilt right side up, align 45-degree angle line of square ruler on seam line to check accuracy. If corner is flat and square, trim excess fabric to 1/4" seam allowance. Press seam open.

 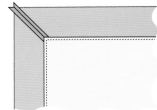

Two Sisters Tip

Border & Block Assembly Pressing Tip

Our favorite tip!

Marrying the border & quilt top is so important for a sharp finished look. It's best to use a flat pressing surface or ironing board when pinning the borders to the quilt. First, find the centers on the quilt & border edges. Place border on the quilt top & PIN to fit within the space. To make sewing easier, use a small burst of steam. The steam will shrink & stretch the fabrics, helping to sandwich the border & quilt top together. Sew & press seam toward border. Do this for all four borders. You will be amazed by the results!

This tip can be used for block assembly too!

Backing

Cut your quilt backing 3" to 5" larger than the quilt top. For large quilts you'll usually have to piece the backing either lengthwise or crosswise. Press the backing fabric before measuring. Always cut the selvages off before sewing the seams together. Use a 1/4" seam allowance and press seams open.

Assembling the Layers

Spread backing, wrong side up, on a flat surface. Anchor it with masking tape or pins being careful not to stretch the backing along the raw edges.

Spread the batting over the backing, smoothing out the wrinkles and lumps.

Place the pressed quilt top over the batting right side up. Make sure the edges are parallel with the edges of the backing fabric to avoid ending up off grain.

Baste the three layers together. Starting in the center each time, baste diagonally to each corner. Continue basting horizontally and vertically until there's enough basting to hold the layers together. You can also use safety pins about 6" to 8" apart instead of basting.

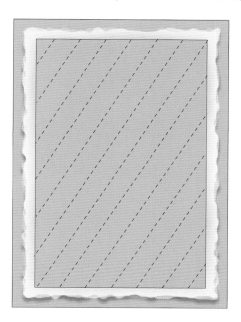

Quilting

All of the quilts shown in this book were machine quilted. Cut batting & backing at least 3" larger than quilt top on all sides. Your quilter will most likely require this.

After quilting, use a rotary cutter to trim backing & batting even with quilt top.

Binding

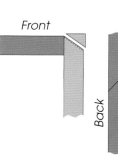

Front

Back

- Place end of two strips per-pendicular to each other forming an 'L', RST. Stitch diagonally & trim to 1/4". Press seam open. Trim the little tri-angle points that stick out.

- Press in half, wrong sides together to form a long strip. It is important that the corners of the quilt be square at 90-degrees.

- Using a 1/4" seam, attach binding using your favorite technique. Hand or machine sews the binding to the reverse side.

If binding a curved edge see instructions for making bias binding on page 9.

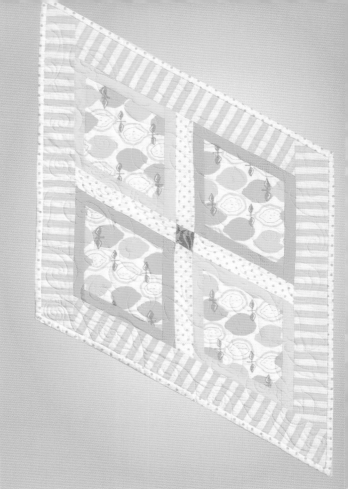

Lemons

The smell of fresh lemons takes me back to fond
childhood memories. I grew up in Northern California
where fresh fruits were abundant. When my mother asked for
a lemon I would run to the backyard and pick the biggest
one off our very own lemon tree.

When I saw this fabric from Alexander Henry it spoke
to me of summer, sweetness and my childhood home.
I can still see myself sitting on our backyard
swing sipping fresh lemonade and daydreaming.
Hummm…it was a wonderful life!

Lemon squares quilt

Finished size: approximately 45·1/2" x 61"

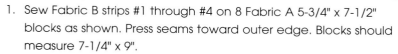

Fabric Requirements

Fabric A	5/8 yard lemon focal for blocks
Fabric B	1/4 yard yellow solid for blocks
Fabric C	1/2 yard orange solid for blocks & inner border
Fabric D	1/4 yard green for appliqué
Fabric E	1-1/8 yards yellow/white dot for blocks, border & binding
Fabric F	1 yard yellow/white stripe for border
Backing	3 yards

Cutting Guide

Fabric A:
- Cut 3 strips 7-1/2" x WOF
  Subcut into 16 blocks 5-3/4" x 7-1/2"

Fabric B:
- Cut 6 strips 1-1/4" x WOF
  Subcut into
  #1—8 strips 1-1/4" x 5-3/4"
  #2—8 strips 1-1/4" x 6-1/2"
  #3—8 strips 1-1/4" x 8-1/4"
  #4—8 strips 1-1/4" x 9"

Fabric C:
- Cut 6 strips 1-1/4" x WOF
  Subcut into
  #1—8 strips 1-1/4" x 5-3/4"
  #2—8 strips 1-1/4" x 6-1/2"
  #3—8 strips 1-1/4" x 8-1/4"
  #4—8 strips 1-1/4" x 9"
- Cut 5 strips 1-1/4" x WOF

Fabric E:
- Cut 1 strip 10" x WOF
  Subcut into 4 blocks 8" x10"
- Cut 4 strips 3-1/4" x WOF
- Cut 6 strips 2-1/4" x WOF

Fabric F:
- Cut 5 strips 6" x WOF

Refer to General Instructions - Appliqué on pages 8-9.

Inner Squares

1. Sew Fabric B strips #1 through #4 on 8 Fabric A 5-3/4" x 7-1/2" blocks as shown. Press seams toward outer edge. Blocks should measure 7-1/4" x 9".

2. Repeat with Fabric C strips #1 through #4 on the remaining 8 Fabric A 5-3/4" x 7-1/2" blocks. Press seams toward outer edge. Blocks should measure 7-1/4" x 9".

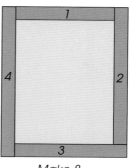

Make 8

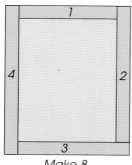

Make 8

Two Sisters Tip

Cutting the background fabric a bit larger than needed is always a good idea when doing appliqué. It is difficult to know how much the fabric may shrink when appliquéing. After appliqué is complete it's easy to cut the square down to the desired size without having to worry if it's going to be large enough.

Appliqué Squares

1. Trace the lemon templates on page 17 onto fusible web. Press fusible web onto the wrong side of Fabric D. Cut out the appliqué shapes on the drawn lines.

2. Center the outer lemon silhouettes on the Fabric E 8" x 10" squares. Add the inner lemon shape and fuse in place.

3. Appliqué using your method of choice.

4. Trim blocks to 7-1/4" x 9" centering the lemon appliqués.

Assembly

1. Assemble rows as shown in the quilt assembly layout.

2. Sew one row at a time. Press seams in opposite directions for each row. Sew rows together to make the quilt center.

Quilt Assembly Layout

Inner Border

Refer to General Instructions - Borders on pages 10-11.

See Two Sisters Tip for Borders on page 11.

1. Measure and cut two side borders from two Fabric E 3-1/4" x WOF strips. These will be the same length. Sew RST to each side of the quilt center. Press seams toward border.

2. Measure and cut a top and bottom border from two Fabric E 3-1/4" x WOF strips. These will be the same length. Sew RST to top and bottom of the quilt center. Press seams toward border.

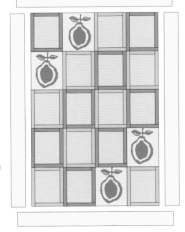

Outer Borders

1. Measure and cut two side borders from two Fabric C 1-1/4" x WOF strips and two Fabric F 6" x WOF strips. These will be the same length. Sew RST. Sew the joined borders to each side of the quilt center, RST. Press seam toward border.

2. Measure and cut a top and bottom border from two Fabric C 1-1/4" x WOF strips and two Fabric F 6" x WOF strips. These will be the same length. Sew RST. Sew the joined borders to the top and bottom of the quilt center, RST. Press seam toward border.

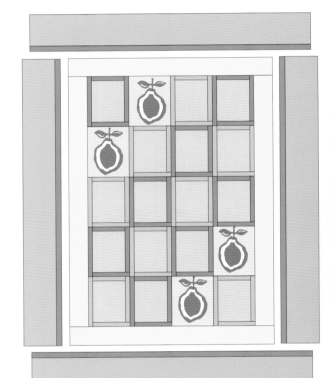

Refer to General Instructions - Backing and Assembling the Layers on page 11.

Quilting

Quilt as desired. Lemon Quilting pattern provided on page 17 can be used for inner square quilting design.

Binding

Refer to General Instructions - Binding on page 11.

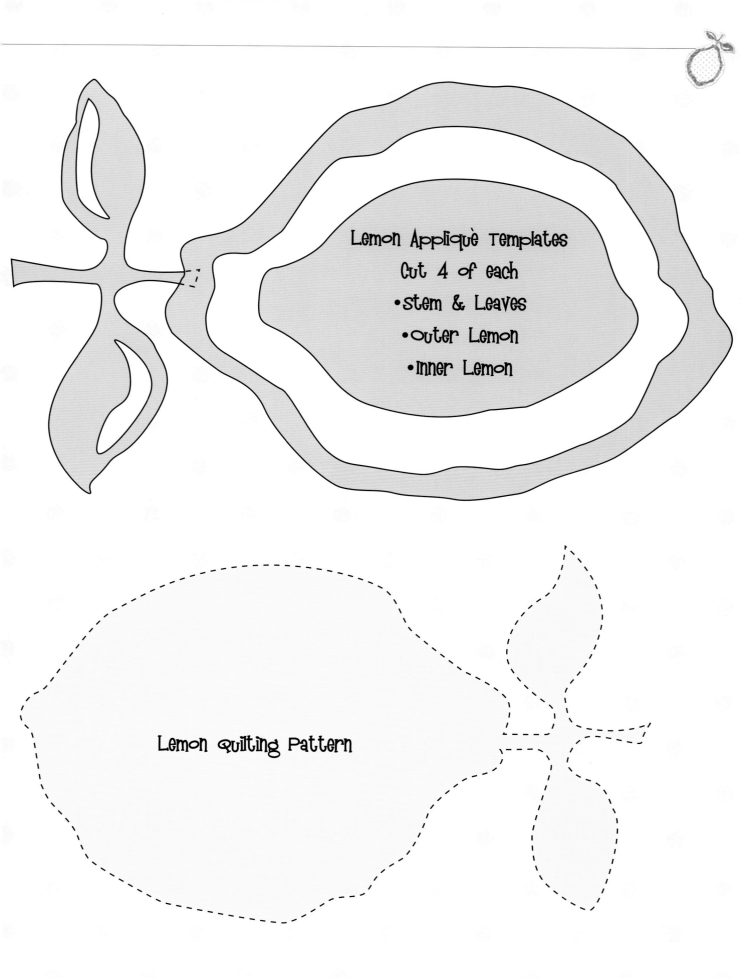

Lemon Appliqué templates
Cut 4 of each
•stem & Leaves
•outer Lemon
•inner Lemon

Lemon Quilting Pattern

Lemon Pillow

Seams to be sewn at 5/8" for this project.

Fabric Requirements

Fabric A	5/8 yard lemon focal for back of pillow, wedges
Fabric B	5 to 7, 10" x 12" pieces assorted fabrics for wedges
Fabric C	1/2 yard yellow/white dot for center gusset & flower leaves
Fabric D	scraps for center of flower
Batting	2, 23" x 23" squares
Zipper	9" zipper
Pom-pom trim	1-3/4 yard
Chenille tape	1/2 yard
Lightweight, non-fusible interfacing	

Cutting Guide

Fabric A:
• Cut 23" x 23" square

Fabric B:
• Cut 16 wedges from the assorted fabrics using template on page 21

Fabric C:
• Cut 2 strips 2-1/2" x WOF
   Sew strips together to make one long strip
   Sub cut into a 62-3/4" strip

Two Sisters Tip

Tracing and cutting templates

When tracing a template it is best to use an extra fine tip Sharpie® marker or thin lead quilting pencil. Using a thin line ensures extra dimensions won't accidently be added to the template. Any extra dimension would throw off the accuracy of the pattern. Trace the template onto Mylar plastic using pencil. Cut out template down the center of the line.
Lay template on fabric and cut with rotary cutter OR draw template shape onto fabric (with a thin line) and cut with rotary cutter and straight edge ruler.

Assembly

1. For front pillow block, lay out 16 wedges in an arrangement of choice.

2. Place two wedges, RST, and sew from the wide edge toward the narrow edge of the wedge. Continue adding wedges until there are 16. Before joining the circle together, press seams open.

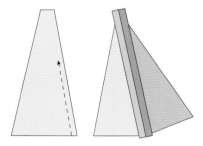

3. Sew the wedge circle together, RST. Press seam.

4. It is rare that this block lies nice and flat. It may need a bit of minor adjusting. Starting at the middle of a wedge and working toward the center, take a slight 1/16" to 1/8" stitch next to the original seam. Go directly across from this seam and repeat the process. Adjusting 2-4 seams is usually all that is needed to have the block lie flat.

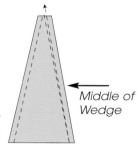

Middle of Wedge

5. Press well and stabilize the fabric before cutting into a circle. Use starch when pressing. This will help stabilize the off-grain fabrics once they are cut into a circle.

6. Fold the wedge block into fourths. Using the Cherry Chef Hat template on page 49, lay it over the wedge block and line up at fold lines. Cut around the template line. Block should measure 20" round.

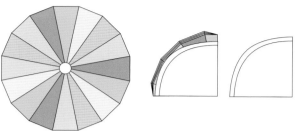

7. Cut the pillow back from Fabric A using the Cherry Chef Hat template on page 49. Circle will measure 20".

Two Sisters Tip

Adding batting to pillow front and back allows the pillow to appear less lumpy when not using a pillow form.

8. Add batting to front and back sides of pillow. Quilt as desired on the front side of the pillow or stitch in the ditch on seam lines. Trim batting to match pillow front.

Flower Leaves

1. Using a 60-degree triangle or the template on page 20, cut 5, Fabric C 5-1/2" 60-degree triangles.

2. Fold down the top corner on each triangle 1/4". Fold and press each side in to make a perfect point.

3. Run a gathering stitch at the lower edge of each leaf.

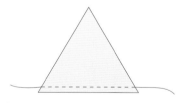

4. Arrange leaves as desired into flower shape layering over and under to form a circle.

5. Refer to General Instructions – Invisible Appliqué on page 9 to appliqué leaves to pillow front.

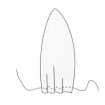

self-faced Flower Center:

1. From a Fabric D scrap, cut a 2-3/4" circle or use template on page 21.

2. Cut 2 pieces 3-1/2" x 3-1/2", one from Fabric D and one from lightweight, non-fusible interfacing

3. Trace template on page 21 onto interfacing.

4. Place interfacing with drawn side up and right side of fabric together. Stitch around circle on the drawn line, gently making curves by lifting the presser foot often to turn corners. Using an open toed appliqué foot helps you see the lines easily.

5. Trim to a scant 1/4" seam allowance. Clip as necessary.

6. Make a small slit in the interfacing and turn circle inside out. Use a stylus or other tool to shape center.

7. Invisible appliqué or use a decorative stitch to stitch flower center onto pillow top.
Optional: Add 2 rows of chenille tape around the center of flower if desired.

Adding Gusset

1. Join the gusset ends together and press seam open.

2. Join the back of pillow and gusset, RST, pinning often and easing in to fit. Mark a 9" space for zipper and baste the seam in this section. Stitch at normal length for remainder of gusset.

3. Following manufacturer's instructions and using a zipper foot, sew in a 9" zipper on seam line of pillow back and gusset using placket method.

4. Using a zipper foot, baste the pom-pom trim onto the edge of pillow with pom-poms facing toward pillow center.

5. Join pillow front to gusset, RST, easing in to fit. Turn inside out.

6. Stuff pillow with filling.

press under 1/4"

Lemon Pillow
Flower Leaf Template
Cut 5

Basting Lines

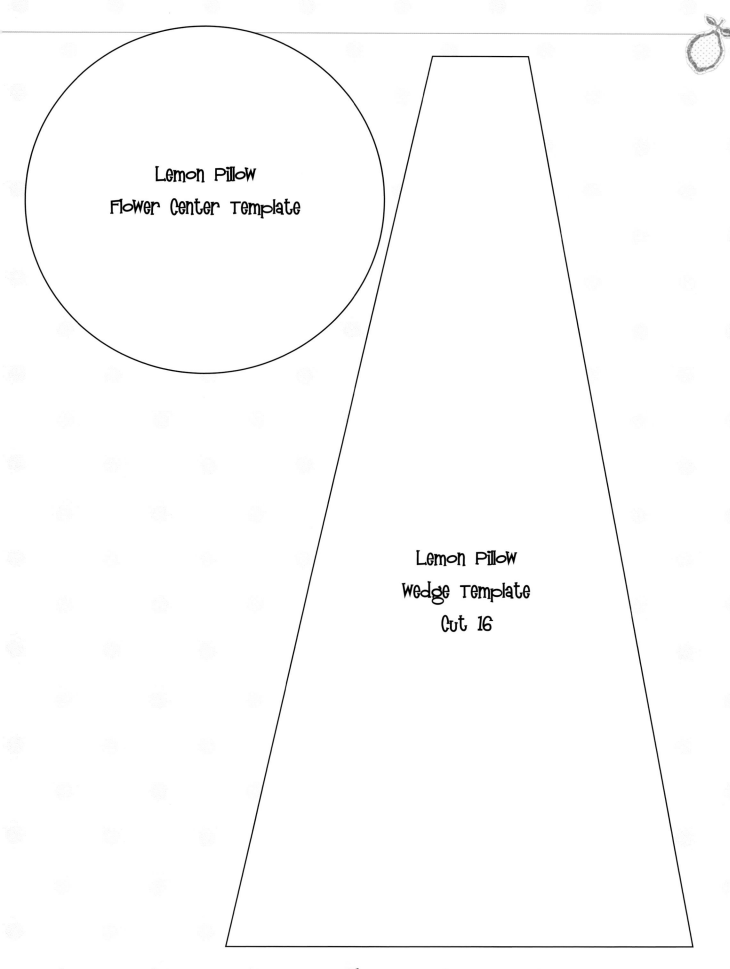

Lemon Pillow
Flower Center Template

Lemon Pillow
Wedge Template
Cut 16

Lemon Place Mat

Finished size: 19-1/2" x 14"

Mom's Best Comfort Food

Bread Pudding with Lemon Sauce

from the kitchen of my dear mother who always had something wonderful waiting for us

Bread Pudding

2 cups day old bread—good quality, not store bought—crusts and all

2 cups milk or half and half

3 T butter

1/4 cup sugar

2 eggs

dash of salt

1/2 cup raisins (slightly boiled and drained)

1/2 tsp vanilla

Cut bread into 1/4 to 1/2 inch cubes. Place in a buttered 1 quart baking dish

Scald the milk with the butter and sugar. Beat the eggs slightly, add salt and stir in the warm milk and the vanilla and drained raisins. Pour over the bread cubes. Set the baking dish in a pan containing warm water up to the level of the pudding and bake in a 350-degree oven for about an hour or until a small knife comes out clean when inserted in the center of pudding. Makes 4-6 servings.

Lemon Sauce

1/2 cup sugar

1-1/2 T cornstarch

1 cup boiling water

2 T butter

1 T grated lemon rind

3 T lemon juice

1/8 tsp salt

Combine sugar and cornstarch; dissolve in boiling water. Cook slowly, stirring constantly, until thickened and clear.

Remove from heat and add remaining ingredients. Serve hot or cold - makes about 1-1/2 cups.

Lemon Place Mat

Makes 1 place mat

Fabric requirements

Fabric A	5 to 7, 4-1/2" x 7" assorted fabrics for wedges
Fabric B	3" x WOF green for inner border & center square
Fabric C	4" x 30" lemon focal for outer border
Fabric D	5" x WOF yellow/white dot for binding
Backing	16" x 22"
Batting	16" x 22"

Cutting Guide

Fabric A:
- Cut 16 wedges using the template on page 24.

Fabric B:
- Cut 2 strips 2-1/4" x 10-1/2"
- Cut 2 strips 1-3/4" x 14"
- Cut 1 piece 2-3/4" x 2-3/4" back with double-sided fusible webbing before cutting

Fabric C:
- Cut 2 strips 3-3/4" x 14"

Fabric D:
- Cut 2 strips 2-1/4" x WOF

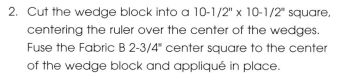

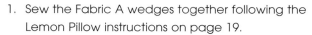

Assembly

1. Sew the Fabric A wedges together following the Lemon Pillow instructions on page 19.

2. Cut the wedge block into a 10-1/2" x 10-1/2" square, centering the ruler over the center of the wedges. Fuse the Fabric B 2-3/4" center square to the center of the wedge block and appliqué in place.

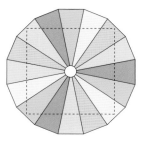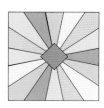

Borders

1. Sew the 2-1/4" x 10-1/2" Fabric B strips to the top and bottom edges of the wedge block. Press seams to outer edge.

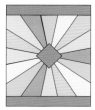

2. Sew the 1-3/4" x 14" Fabric B strips to the sides of the wedge block. Press seams to outer edge.

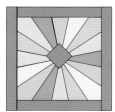

3. Sew the 3-3/4" x 14" Fabric C strips to either side of the wedge block. Press seams to outer edge.

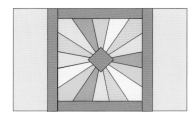

Refer to General Instructions - Backing and Assembling the Layers on page 11.

Quilt as desired.

Refer to General Instructions - Binding on page 11.

Lemon Place Mat

Lemon Place Mat
Wedge Template
Cut 16

Lemon Dishtowel

Required Ingredients

- Approximately 20" x 28" purchased dishtowel
- Template below for lemon appliqué
- 22" pom-pom trim

Refer to General Instructions - Appliqué on pages 8-9.

1. Trace the lemon templates below onto fusible web.

2. Measure 3-3/4" up from lower edge of the dishtowel. Center and fuse the lemon background and lemon into place. Appliqué using method of choice.

3. Measure 2" from lower edge of dishtowel. Place top of pom-pom trim on this line and sew into place, turning under edges on the reverse side of dishtowel.

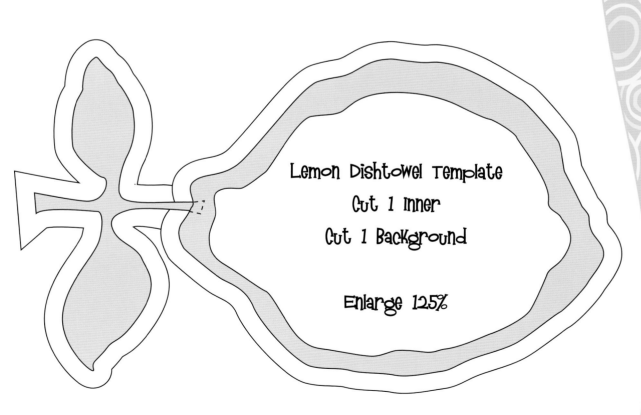

Lemon Dishtowel Template

Cut 1 Inner

Cut 1 Background

Enlarge 125%

Lemon Napkin Ring & Napkins

Finished napkin size:
approximately 18-1/4" x 18-1/4"

Lemon Napkin Ring

Fabric Requirements

Fabric A 2, 4" x 4" white/yellow dot squares for flower

Fabric B 2, 2-1/2" x 2-1/2" yellow/white dot squares for flower center

Fabric C 2, 4" x 4-1/2" green pieces for leaves

Fabric D 3/4" x WOF lemon focal strip for napkin ring cover; cut with a pinking blade

Batting 2-1/2" x 2-1/2" square for flower center

Napkin rings

1" in diameter with a flat bottom. The flat bottom and width offer more support for this design.

Lemon Napkins

Makes 1 napkin

Fabric Requirements

Fabric A 18" x 18" square of lemon focal for napkin center

Fabric B 1-1/2" x WOF light green for binding

Instructions

Refer to General Instructions – Binding on page 11.

Sew Fabric B binding strip on the Fabric A napkin center using a decorative stitch if desired.

Instructions for Lemon Nakin Ring

Flower & Leaves

1. Iron a 3-1/2" x 3-1/2" square of fusible web to the wrong side of a 4" x 4" Fabric A square. Peel off the paper and place remaining 4" x 4" Fabric A square wrong side down on top of web. Iron the two squares together.

2. Trace the flower template on one side of the fused fabric squares and cut out.

3. Trace the flower center template on the wrong side of a 2-1/2" x 2-1/2" Fabric B square. Cut a small X in the center for turning. With the Fabric B squares RST, place the batting on the bottom of the 2 squares. Sew a circle in the center. Clip curves, turn inside out, and press well. Topstitch in circles on top of flower center.

4. Trace the leaf template on the wrong side of a 4" x 4-1/2" Fabric C piece. Cut a short line down the center of the leaf for turning. Stitch around the shape, trim, and clip curves. Turn inside out and press well. Fuse, glue, or whip stitch the slit closed.

5. Run a basting stitch in a matching thread color down the center of the leaf. Pull thread to create a small gather and tie off to secure.

6. Repeat to make a second leaf.

7. Tightly wrap the Fabric D 3/4" x WOF strip around the napkin ring. Glue to secure.

Assembly

Place Liquid Stitch® or fabric glue on the back side of the flower at the center. Place the two leaves on the back side of flower making sure the leaves stick out past the flower. Place on top of the napkin ring. Attach flower center with glue.

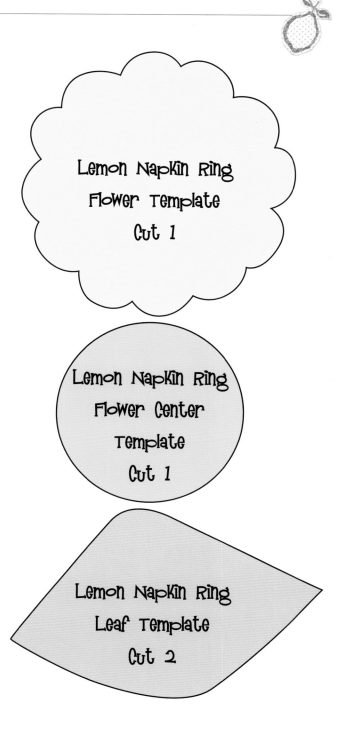

Lemon Napkin Ring Flower Template Cut 1

Lemon Napkin Ring Flower Center Template Cut 1

Lemon Napkin Ring Leaf Template Cut 2

Lemon Table Topper

Finished size: approximately 23-1/2" x 28"

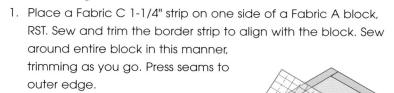

Fabric Requirements

Fabric A	1/4 yard lemon focal for inner squares
Fabric B	1/4 yard white/yellow dot for sashing & binding
Fabric C	1/8 yard yellow solid for inner square borders
Fabric D	1/8 yard orange solid for inner square borders
Fabric E	1/4 yard yellow/white stripe for outer border
Fabric F	scrap green accent for center square
Backing	7/8 yard

Cutting Guide

Fabric A:
• Cut 4 blocks using template on page 31.

Fabric B:
• Cut 2 sashing 1 strips using template on page 30.
• Cut 2 sashing 2 strips using template on page 30.
• Cut 2 strips 2-1/4" x WOF

From Fabric C:
• Cut 2 strips 1-1 /4" x WOF

Fabric D:
• Cut 2 strips 1-1 /4" x WOF

Fabric E:
• Cut 2 strips 3" x WOF

Fabric F:
• Cut center square using template on page 30.

Inner squares

1. Place a Fabric C 1-1/4" strip on one side of a Fabric A block, RST. Sew and trim the border strip to align with the block. Sew around entire block in this manner, trimming as you go. Press seams to outer edge.

2. Repeat with the remaining Fabric C 1-1/4" strip and a Fabric A block for a total of 2 blocks.

3. Place a Fabric D 1-1/4" strip on one side of a Fabric A block, RST. Sew and trim the border strip to align with the block. Sew around entire block in this manner, trimming as you go. Press seams to outer edge.

4. Repeat with the remaining Fabric D 1-1/4" strip and Fabric A block for a total of 2 blocks.

5. Lay out the four blocks with Fabric B sashing strips in between. Join two blocks with a sashing strip to form a row. Press seams to outer edge. Make two rows.

6. Add center sashing strips to Fabric F center square. Press seams toward sashing strips.

7. Sew the two rows together with sashing strip in the middle to form the table topper center. Press seams toward sashing strip.

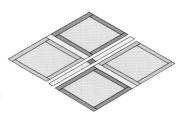

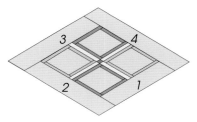

Border

Sew the Fabric E 3" strips to the table topper center to form the outer border. Add the strips in numerical order as shown. Trim off excess as you go.

Refer to General Instructions - Backing and Assembling the Layers on page 11.

Quilting

Quilt as desired.

Binding

Refer to General Instructions - Binding on page 11.

Lemon Table
Topper
Sashing 1
Template
Cut 2

Lemon Table
Topper
Sashing 2
Template
Cut 2

Lemon Table
Topper
Center square
Template
Cut 1

Lemon Table Topper

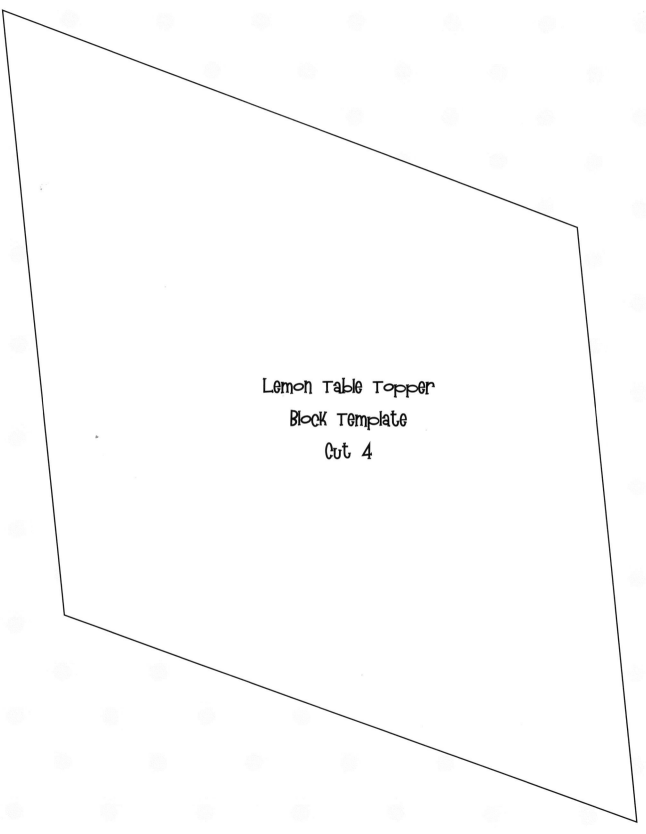

Lemon Table Topper
Block Template
Cut 4

Cherries

Red and Aqua are two colors that combine so perfectly &
they happen to be two of my favorite fabric combinations.

My childhood home was surrounded by cherry orchards.
There were fresh cherries everywhere around us.
I loved the cherry fabric from Robert Kaufman used in this
collection and wanted to use their fresh take on a great fruit
to make a children's kitchen collection.
I hope you get the same feeling I do when you look at it.

I can't help but smile and think of my darling little gran-girls
running around in the kitchen helping mom… or ME!
Can't you just imagine the treat that's waiting for you?

sweet Cherry scalloped quilt

Finished size: approximately 42" x 42"

Fabric Requirements

Fabric A   1-3/8 yards focal print for border & inner blocks

Fabric B   3/8 yard aqua dot for contrasting outer triangles & center circle

Fabric C   5/8 yard white for sixteen patch & inner square

Fabric D   1/4 yard aqua print for sixteen patch

Fabric E   1/4 yard red print for red star

Fabric F   1/2 yard solid red for appliqué & binding

1-1/4" Jumbo Rick Rack   3-1/2 yards

Backing   2-3/4 yards

TOOLS:

1" bias tape maker

Mylar plastic for making templates

Cutting Guide

Fabric A:

Refer to layout diagram for placement before cutting.

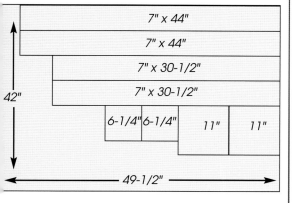

- Cut 2 squares 11-1/2" x 11-1/2"
- Cut 4 squares 6-1/4" x 6-1/4"
  Subcut in half diagonally
  to make 8 triangles

- Cut 2 strips 7" x 30-1/2" on length of grain
- Cut 2 strips 7" x 44" on length of grain
See Two Sisters tip on Borders on page 11.

Fabric B:
- Cut 2 squares 11-1/2" x 11-1/2"
- Cut 1 square 8-1/2" x 8-1/2"

Fabric C:
- Cut 3 strips 2-1/2" x WOF
- Cut 1 square 12" x 12"

Fabric D:
- Cut 3 strips 2-1/2" x WOF

Fabric E:
- Cut 4 squares 6-1/4" x 6-1/4"
  Subcut in half diagonally to make 8 triangles

Fabric F:
- Cut one 7" x 9" square for appliqué
- Cut one 18" x 18" square for binding

Sixteen Patch Blocks

Two Sisters Tip

When sewing long strips of fabric together it is helpful to cut the length into 2 pieces if the project allows. This helps eliminate the "wave" that can often occur when piecing long strips together. For this project cutting the strips in half is recommended.

1. Cut the 2-1/2" strips from Fabric C and Fabric D in half on the fabric fold.

2. Sew a 2-1/2" C and D fabric strip RST. Repeat for remaining strips. Press to dark fabric.

3. Cut into 2-1/2" wide two patch units.

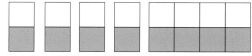

Make 64

Two Sisters Tip

Chain Piecing

The fastest way to piece a large number of blocks is to join them together at the same time without stopping to cut threads. Place the first two pieces of fabric to be joined under the presser foot and sew from edge to edge. Feed the next two pieces without cutting your thread, until all pieces have been joined. Cut threads to separate.

4. Sew 2, two patch units into a four patch unit nesting seams together. Press seams to one side. Repeat to make 16 four patch units.

Make 16

5. Sew 4, four patch units together to make 1, 7-1/2" x 7-1/2" square. Press seams. Repeat to make 4 sixteen patch blocks.

Make 4

Adding Outer Corners

1. Find the center of each Fabric A and E triangle and gently finger press to create a guide mark.

2. Lay out the 4, sixteen patch blocks in the same direction with an aqua print fabric square at the top of the unit.

3. With RST sew 2 Fabric A triangles to the sixteen patch block. Press seams toward the outer edge of the block.

4. Repeat with 2 Fabric E triangles on the remaining sides. Trim to a 10-1/2" x 10-1/2" square centering the sixteen patch block in the middle. Press seams toward the outer edge of the block.

Half-square Triangle Blocks

1. On the wrong side of the 11-1/2" Fabric A squares draw a line from corner to corner with a quilter's pencil or chalk pen.

2. Lay an 11-1/2" Fabric A square on an 11-1/2" Fabric B square, RST. Stitch 1/4" on both sides of the drawn line. Cut down the center line and press to the dark fabric. Trim to a 10-1/2" x 10-1/2" square.

Make 4

Center Appliqué

Refer to General Instructions - Appliqué on pages 8-9.

Two Sisters Tip

Cutting the background fabric a bit larger than needed is always a good idea when doing appliqué. It is difficult to know how much the fabric may shrink when appliquéing. After appliqué is complete it's easy to cut the block down to the desired size without having to worry if it's going to be large enough.

1. From the 8-1/2" Fabric B square cut a 7-1/2" circle. Press fusible web onto the wrong side of the fabric. Cut out the appliqué shape on the drawn line.

2. Fold the circle in fourths and gently pinch the edges to create a crease. This will serve as a guide for placement.

3. Fold the white 12" x 12" square in half and then in half again, dividing it into fourths. Gently pinch the edges to create a crease. Match the Fabric B circle crease lines to these lines 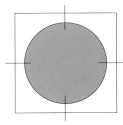 and press to fuse, following the manufacturer's instructions. Appliqué the circle to the center block using your method of choice.

4. Trace the cherry template on page 40 onto fusible web. Press fusible web onto the wrong side of the Fabric F scrap. Cut out the appliqué shape on the drawn line.

5. Fuse the cherry to the circle referring to the photograph on page 41 for placement. Appliqué using your method of choice.

6. Trim the square to 10-1/2" x 10-1/2", centering the design.

Assembly

1. Refer to General Instructions - Borders on pages 10-11 before beginning.

2. Join the 10-1/2" squares together in rows as shown. Press seams in alternate directions in each row. Join rows together to make the quilt center.

3. Fold each of the Fabric A 7" x 30-1/2" border pieces in half to find the center. Place one on the quilt's top edge, RST, matching the centers. Pin and sew in place. Repeat for the quilt's bottom edge.

4. Repeat for each of the Fabric A 7" x 44" side border pieces. Press all seams to outer edge of quilt.

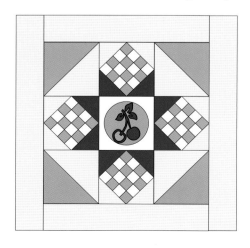

scalloped Border

Two Sisters Tip

When marking any fabric it is always best to try out your marking pen or pencil on a scrap of the fabric you are using. Hand wash the sample to ensure it will not be permanent on your project. This way you will know if this marker will work on your fabric and you won't be disappointed if the marks don't wash out.

NOTE: When making a scalloped border the scallops are drawn on before quilting. This way when you or your quilter quilts the project, you will know where the border will end. This will also be the guideline for sewing on the binding.

1. Trace scallops on pages 38-39 onto template plastic and cut out or use your favorite scallop template.

2. To mark scallops on cherry border, measure 2-1/4" down from each border's seam line. Mark points with a marker at several points across length of all border edges. Now measure approximately 3/4" from border edges and mark with lines.

3. Place one corner of the 9" scallop template on these lines and mark the first scallop. Repeat this eight times for outer scallops at all border edges.

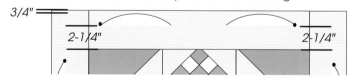

4. Add inner 7" scallop in between the 2, 9" scallops. Make adjustments to scallop length with 7" scallop if necessary.

Corner scallops

1. At one corner of quilt begin marking a corner scallop by laying a straight ruler across the inner quilt corner and the outer border of the diagonal on the corner. Measure out 7-1/2" and mark this point. Place the edge of an 8" circle or plate on the corner mark. Mark a half circle on the quilt. Join the corner scallop to the two outer 9" scallops to complete the four corner scallops on the quilt.

STOP: Do not cut on the marked line! You must

Quilting

Quilt as desired. A cherry quilting template pattern is provided on page 40.

Scalloped Binding

1. A bias binding is an absolute must for curved edges! A narrow single-fold bias binding is required. Make approximately 185" of bias binding. Refer to General Instructions - Bias Binding on page 9.

2. Using a 1" bias tape maker, follow manufacturer's instructions to make single fold bias tape.

Adding the Binding

1. Before binding, machine baste along the marked edge of the scalloped border. This will keep the edges from stretching or shifting as you sew on the binding. You can now trim a few inches away from the scalloped edge to eliminate bulk when sewing on the binding. On the inside of the scallops, clip and trim a small bit into the point allowing the quilt to stretch flat when the binding is sewn on.

2. Working on the front side of the quilt, position the binding on the quilt top with all raw edges even.

3. Leave a 10" tail before beginning to sew. This will ensure you have adequate binding to join on the curve. Using a walking foot is ideal for sewing the binding to the quilt. Open the binding and beginning in the center of a scallop sew the binding to the quilt top catching only a single side of the binding.

4. Sew using a 1/4" seam. Ease the binding around the curves. Stitch to the base of the V, stop with the needle down at that point. Lift the presser foot, pivot the quilt and binding to begin sewing out of the V. Put the presser foot down and sew out of the V, taking care not to stitch any pleats in the binding. Lift the presser foot and pivot the quilt and binding until the binding edge is again even with the marked line on the quilt. Lower the presser foot and continue stitching around the quilt. Join the binding ends to complete the binding.

5. Trim the excess batting and backing at the edge of the binding. Turn the binding to the back side of the quilt. Stitch down by hand. The binding will fold over itself at the inside corners like a reverse mitered corner.

Adding Trim

1. After the binding is complete add the rick rack around the center. Starting at one corner center the rick rack over the seam line. Sew the rick rack around the center, mitering at the corners. Trim the excess rick rack and sew the end in place.

Two Sisters Tip

Using invisible thread is a terrific way to add trim to any project. When using a wide trim it allows one to sew on both sides of the trim preventing it from curling up after washing. This is the perfect project to try your hand with invisible thread. The tension on your machine may need to be loosened just a bit. Practice using the thread before adding trim to your project.

7" border scallops

Cut 1

Draw 4

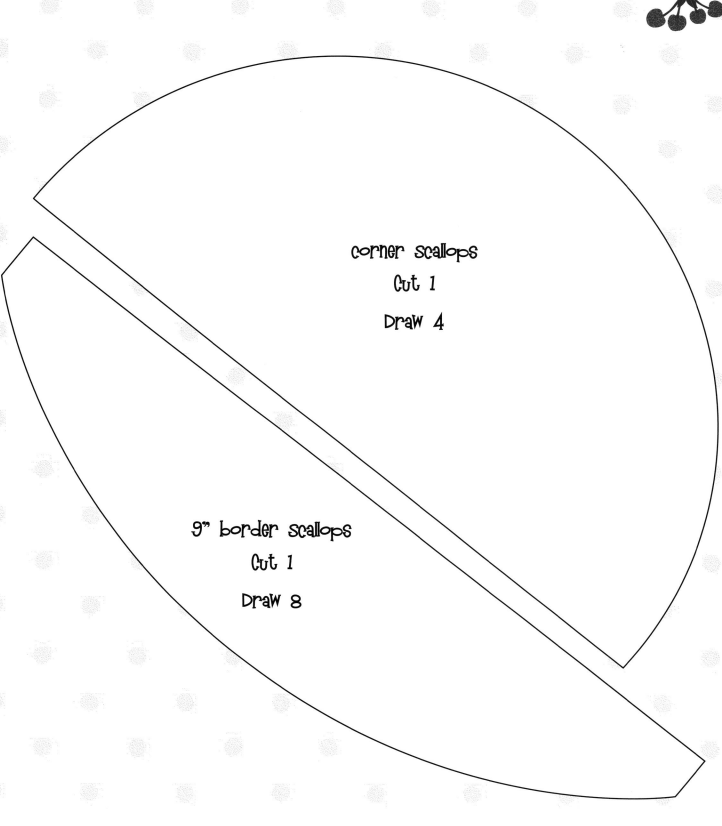

corner scallops

Cut 1

Draw 4

9" border scallops

Cut 1

Draw 8

cherry Template
for Center Block
Cut 1

Cherry quilting
pattern

sweet Cherry scalloped Quilt

so sweet
Cherry Apron

Fabric Requirements

Apron pattern sizes fit 2T-5T

Fabric A	3/4 yard focal print for apron, chef hat, & oven mitt
Fabric B	1/2 yard red print for apron
Fabric C	3/8 yard aqua print for apron
Fabric D	1/8 yard white with red circles for chef hat
Assorted	18, 1-1/2" strips for oven mitt & kitchen tool tote

2"-wide Velcro 4"

Scrap flowers

3/4" buttons 2

Bias tape 5"

1-1/4" rick rack trim 1/2 yard

12" zipper for tote

Lining	20" x 20" for tote
Batting	20" x 20" for tote

Two Sisters Tip

Got to have it Tools! *A rolled hemming foot is a wonderful tool for any project requiring a neat finished edge. This foot paired with a gathering foot will save you time and frustration when making yards of ruffles. When making children's clothing or decorative projects for your home, these are must have sewing feet!*

However, if a gathering foot is unavailable, use dental floss and zig-zag over the top, making sure not to catch the floss. This makes a great way to gather effectively without using specialized feet.

Cutting Guide

Refer to pages 45-47 for pocket, bodice, and neck strap patterns.

Fabric A:
- Cut 2 strips 2-1/2" x 26" for size 2-3T OR
  Cut 2 strips 2-1/2" x 30" for size 4-5T for apron strings
- Cut 4 neck strap pieces - 2 for apron, 2 for lining from neck strap template on page 46 or 47
- Cut 1, 10" x 18" piece for size 2-3T OR
  Cut 1, 12" x 20" piece for size 4-5T for apron body
  Sub cut apron body as shown:

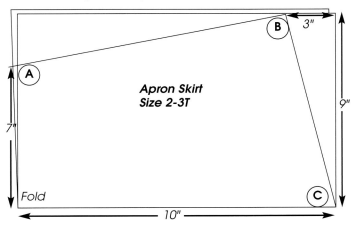

A Measure 7" (2-3T) or 7-1/2" (4-5T) from fold line and mark.

B Measure 3" from lower edge of fabric on selva ge edge. Mark.
Draw a line from point A to B and cut on line.

C Draw line from point B to C and cut on line.

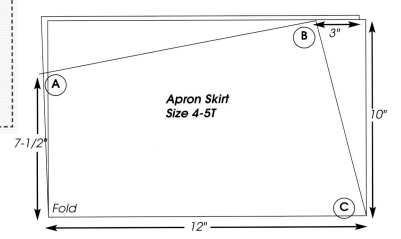

Fabric B:
- Cut 1 strip 3-1/4" x WOF
- Cut 2 pieces RST, from bodice template on page 46-47
- Cut 1 square 5-1/2" x 5-1/2"

Fabric C:
- Cut 2 pieces RST, from bodice template on page 46-47
- Cut 1 square 5-1/2" x 5-1/2".

Apron strings

1. Narrowly hem down one side of the 2-1/2" Fabric A strips, turning under all raw edges.

2. Fold back the hemmed edge RST to form a triangle at one end. Stitch across to the point. Clip and turn right side out, using a tool to poke out the corner.

3. Narrowly hem remaining raw edge and press.

Assembly of Bodice

1. Place Fabrics B and C, RST. Using the templates on pages 46-47, cut 2 bodice pieces from each fabric.

2. Lay out Fabric A, RST. Place the templates on pages 46-47 on fabric and cut out two neck strap pieces.

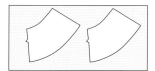

3. Stitch one neck strap piece to one of each color bodice front at shoulder. Press seams open.

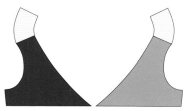

4. With RST, stitch bodice lining to bodice front at neck and armhole edges. Trim seam and clip curves. Turn inside out and press well.

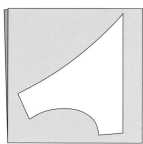

5. Baste apron strings to front bodice pieces, pleating the tie to fit within dots.

6. Open bodice at side seams and with RST stitch side seam from lower edge of bodice to edge of lining. Reinforce over apron string. Turn right side out and press.

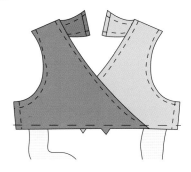

7. Topstitch neck and armhole edges 1/4" from edge, turning in neck strap ends 1/2".

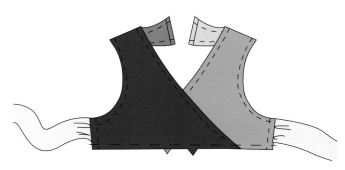

8. Lap right front over left matching centers front notches with raw edges even. Baste at lower edge.

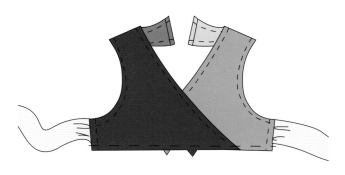

Pocket

1. Using the template below, trace the pattern onto the wrong side of the Fabric B, 5-1/2" square. Place the Fabric B and Fabric D, 5-1/2" square pieces RST and sew leaving an opening between the dots. Clip curves, turn inside out, and press. Slip stitch the seam closed. Press well. Press top of pocket down on fold line.

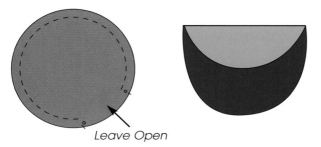

Leave Open

Ruffle

1. Hem all sides of the Fabric B, 3-1/4" strip turning in all raw edges.

2. On back side of strip, measure down 5/8". Using the guide on your sewing machine, sew a gathering stitch. Pull gathers on strip to form a ruffle to fit lower edge of apron.

Apron Body

1. Overcast or serge the lower edge of the apron body to finish.

2. Hem the sides of apron turning in all raw edges. Press under 1/4" and turn under once more. Stitch.

3. Place gathered ruffle on top of the right side of apron 1/2" from edge. Pin into place dividing gathers evenly. Stitch on gathered line to secure.

4. Place pocket on front of apron and angle as desired. Stitch in place being sure to reinforce the top of the pocket with backstitching.

5. Attach the bodice front to the apron body, RST. Pin and stitch. Overcast edges. Press seam toward apron body.

6. Add Velcro® at the two neck edges for closure.

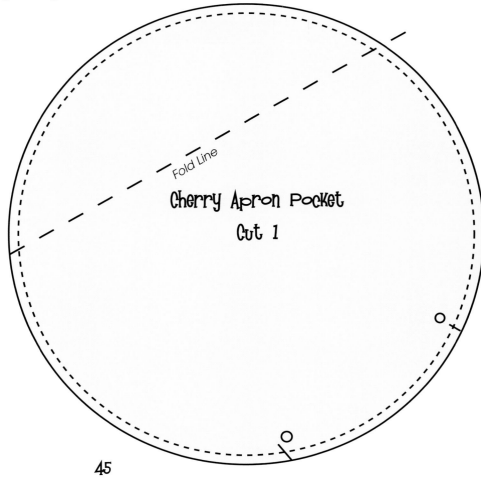

Fold Line

Cherry Apron Pocket

Cut 1

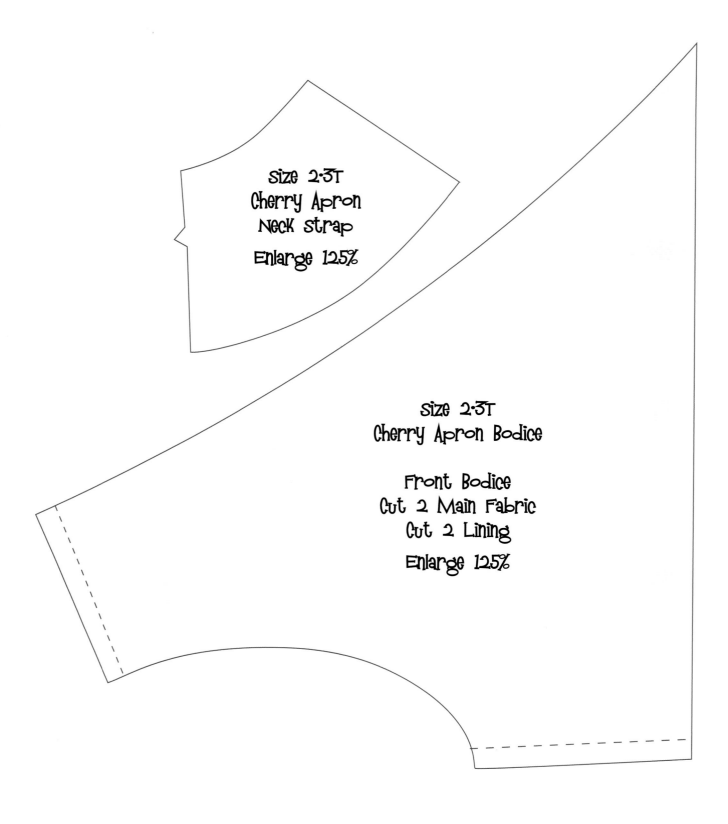

Size 2-3T
Cherry Apron
Neck strap

Enlarge 125%

Size 2-3T
Cherry Apron Bodice

Front Bodice
Cut 2 Main Fabric
Cut 2 Lining

Enlarge 125%

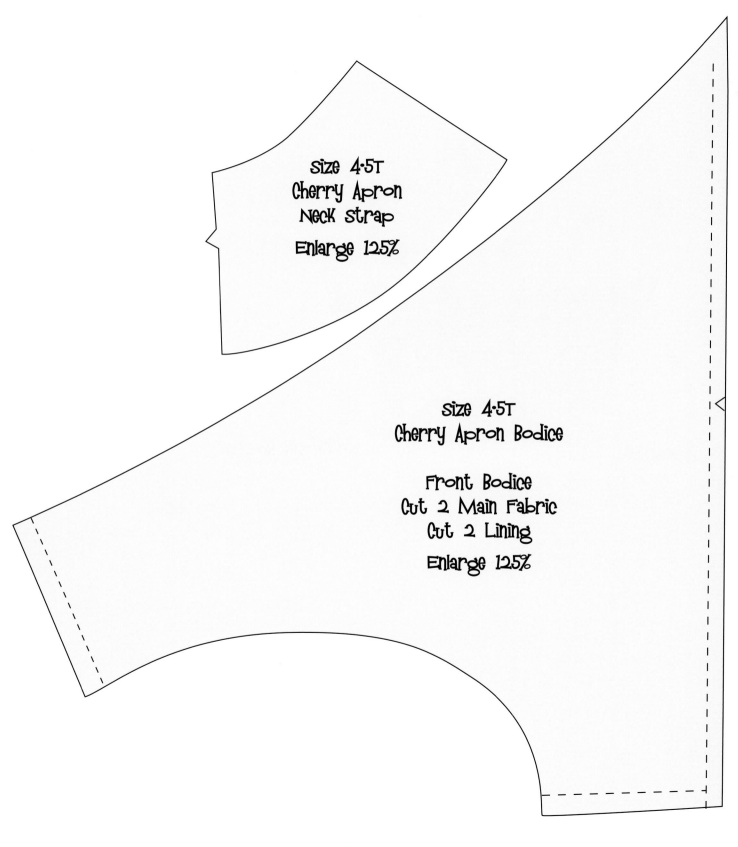

size 4·5T
Cherry Apron
Neck Strap

Enlarge 125%

size 4·5T
Cherry Apron Bodice

Front Bodice
Cut 2 Main Fabric
Cut 2 Lining

Enlarge 125%

Cherry Chef's Hat

Fabric Requirements

Fabric A	22" x 22" square focal fabric
Fabric B	6" x 23" white with red circles for Size 2-3T OR 6" x 24-1/2" for Size 4-5T
Scrap	Aqua-print for flower
Interfacing	22" x 22" square 3" x 23" for Size 2-3T OR 3" x 24-1/2" for Size 4-5T

Assembly

1. Following manufacturer's instructions, iron the 22" x 22" square of interfacing onto the hat's main fabric.

2. Fold the fabric into fourths. Cut into a circle using the template on page 49. Cut out using rotary cutter along the outside edge.

3. Measure 2" up from the outside edge and mark with a drawn line. Cut out on line with scissors. With bias or seam tape, sew RST onto the edge of the slit opening, turning at center point. Press tape to inside edge. Stitch in place. This will allow the hat to fit multiple sizes and allow for growth.

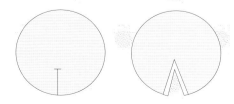

4. Using a basting stitch and a gathering foot, if available, gather the circle to measure approx 23" for size 2-3T and 24-1/2" for size 4-5T

Preparing the Band

1. Iron the size of interfacing needed (see sizing in fabric requirements) onto one side of the band on the wrong side of fabric.

2. Fold band in half, RST, and sew down each short end to within 1/2" of the raw edge. Backstitch.

Fold

48

3. Turn band inside out and press. With a pencil or fabric marker, make a mark 2" in from one end and 1/2" away from the raw edge. This will become the closure for the hat.

4. With RST and starting with slit opening of hat (see step 3, Assembly), pin hat to one raw edge of band, easing in fullness between the 2" mark and opposite end of band. Sew, using a 1/2" seam. Press hat seam to inside of band. Fold the remaining raw edge 1/2" along length of band. Hand sew or topstitch the hat to the band. Add Velcro® to the 2" hat tab for closure.

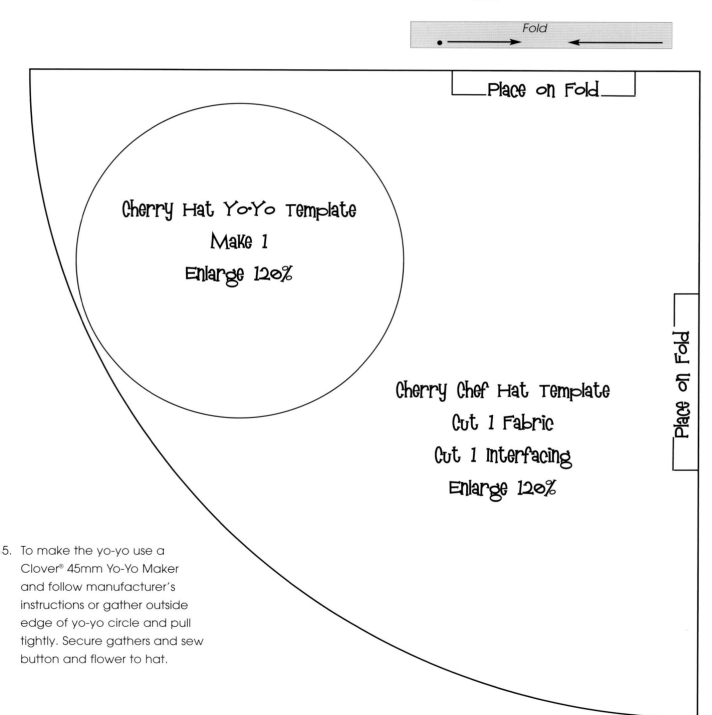

Place on Fold

Cherry Hat Yo-Yo Template
Make 1
Enlarge 120%

Cherry Chef Hat Template
Cut 1 Fabric
Cut 1 Interfacing
Enlarge 120%

Place on Fold

5. To make the yo-yo use a Clover® 45mm Yo-Yo Maker and follow manufacturer's instructions or gather outside edge of yo-yo circle and pull tightly. Secure gathers and sew button and flower to hat.

Cherry Oven Mitt

Fabric Requirements

Fabric A   1/4 yard for top half of oven mitt

Assorted   1-1/2" strips or honey bun strips for lower mitt

Batting   2, 6" x 8-1/2" pieces

Cutting Guide

Fabric A:
- Cut 2 pieces 5-1/2" x 5-1/2"
- Cut one strip 1-1/4" x 2-1/2"
- Cut 2 pieces from template on page 51 for mitt lining

Assorted 1-1/2" strips:
- Cut 12 assorted pieces 4-1/2" long

Assembly

Lower Mitt

1. Sew 12, 1-1/2" strips RST together, alternating fabrics, to form one piece of fabric. Press all seams in the same direction.

2. Use the template on page 51 and pin into place on the fabric. Cut out two pieces for the lower half of mitt.

Upper Mitt

1. Place Fabric A, 5-1/2" squares RST and cut out two pieces using the template on page 51.

2. Sew the lower and upper mitt sections together for outer mitt. Press seams to top of mitt.

3. Press the 1-1/4" x 2-1/2" Fabric A strip under 1/4" on each side; fold in half. Stitch. Fold in half again to make a side loop. Place on side of mitt where marked with dot.

4. Lay out front and back mitt pieces right sides up on top of batting. Baste and trim batting to fabric edge. Pin the two sides of mitt RST and sew around the entire mitt except at lower edge. Trim and clip at corners turning inside out.

5. Using the two lining pieces, sew to make a second mitt omitting the batting. Do not turn inside out.

6. Place lining and mitt lower edges RST. Place the lining inside the mitt. Stitch at lower edge leaving a 3" opening. Trim and turn inside out. Topstitch and press at lower edge to finish.

This mitt is designed for play purposes only. If it is desired for real kitchen use, purchase Insul–Brite® batting & follow manufacturer's directions for assembly.

Loop placement

Cherry Oven Mitt
Top section Template
Cut 2
Enlarge 120%

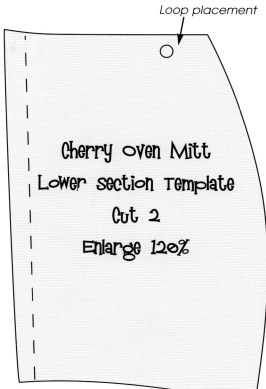

Cherry Oven Mitt
Lower section Template
Cut 2
Enlarge 120%

Cherry Oven Mitt
Lining Template
Cut 2
Enlarge 120%

Cherry Tool Tote

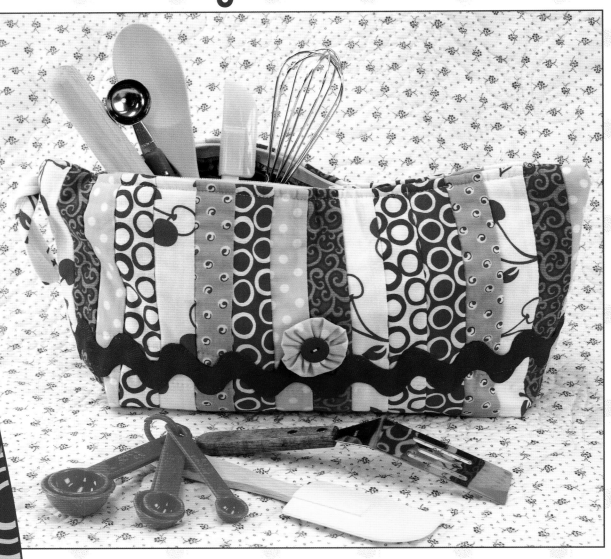

Fabric requirements

Fabric A	approximately 16 assorted 1-1/2" strips or honey bun strips
Fabric B	fat quarter for lining
Batting	18" x 20-1/2"

Cutting Guide:

Fabric A:
- Cut 16 assorted strips to measure 1-1/2" x 20" Subcut one strip 1-1/2" x 8" for bag handle

Creating the Fabric one strip at a time

The bag is made from 1-1/2" strips. To create the outer bag fabric and the lining at the same time:

1. Place the Fabric B fat quarter right side down.

2. Place batting on top of the fat quarter. Baste around edges to secure.

3. Place 2, Fabric A 1-1/2" x 20" strips, RST, on top of batting. Stitch together on one long edge, sewing through all layers. Press strips open.

4. Continue to add one strip at a time. This will quilt the fabrics as you go.

5. Trim fabric piece to measure 16-1/2" x 19". Overcast all edges.

Assembly

1. Measure 5-1/2" down from one side of the 16" width of bag. Draw a placement line across the bag. Place top of rick rack trim on this line and stitch in place. Refer to the Adding Trim Tip in Sweet Cherry Scalloped Quilt on page 38.

2. With RST, fold bag in half matching strips. Mark 1-1/2" in from both outer edges and sew a 3/4" seam using a normal length stitch. Baste the remaining 13" center seam, easing to fit. Press open.

Baste

3. Following manufacturer's instructions, put in zipper using a center placement method.

4. Turn bag inside out. Using the 1-1/2" x 8" Fabric A strip, press 1/4" on both sides. Fold in half and stitch. Fold loop in half and baste at side seam 3/4" down from top edge of bag. Place side seams RST and stitch down from top seam to lower edge on both sides.

Squarely Boxing the Corners

1. To box the bottom of the bag, work with the bag inside out. With the bag in an upright position, align the sewn side seam with the center bottom of the bag. Make sure the seam is truly centered by measuring with a ruler.

2. Measure 2" from the point. Draw a straight line across bottom at this measurement and pin in place. Make sure the fabric on the left and right side of seam are the same measurement. Sew on line. Trim seam to 1/4" and overcast edges. Repeat for other bag corner.

Yo-Yo

1. See Cherry Chef Hat for instructions on making a yo-yo to decorate the tote. Sew in center of the bag on rick rack trim, add button.

Fill bag with Children's Kitchen Tools from Sassyfrass Enterprises, www.sassyfrassenterprises.com.

Cherry Dishtowel

Required ingredients:

Approximately 20" x 28" purchased dishtowel

Template on page 55 for cherry appliqué

7" x 7" fabric for circle

Scraps for cherry & stem

22", 5/8" rick rack trim

Assembly

Refer to General Instructions - Appliqué on pages 8-9.

1. Measure 4-1/2" up from lower edge of dishtowel. Center and fuse the background circle and cherry in place. Appliqué using your method of choice.

2. Measure 2-1/2" from lower edge of dishtowel and mark. Place rick rack trim on this mark and sew into place turning under edges on reverse side.

Cherry Tarts   So Delicious!

from the kitchen of Meg Miles, my darling daughter!

1/2 cup butter, softened

2 cups powdered sugar

1 tsp baking powder

1/2 tsp salt

1 tsp vanilla

1 tsp almond extract

1 egg

2-1/2 cups flour

48 red maraschino cherries, drained

1/2 cup coarse sugar

For a special Christmas cookies add 1/2 cup finely crushed peppermint candies and use 1 tsp peppermint extract instead of almond extract.

Preheat oven to 350-degrees. In a large mixing bowl beat butter on medium to high speed for 30 seconds. Gradually beat in 1-1/2 cups of powdered sugar, the baking powder, and salt. Beat in almond extract, vanilla, and egg. Beat in as much of the flour as you can before it gets too stiff, then complete stirring in the flour by hand.

Place remaining 1/2 cup powdered sugar in a shallow dish. Shape dough into 1" balls. Roll in sugar. Press each ball into the sides and bottom of a small muffin cup. Place cherry in each cup. Bake for 10-12 minutes or until partially browned. Sprinkle with coarse sugar. Carefully transfer to rack to cool completely.

To store:
Place in a single layer and cover in an airtight container. Can be refrigerated for 3 days.

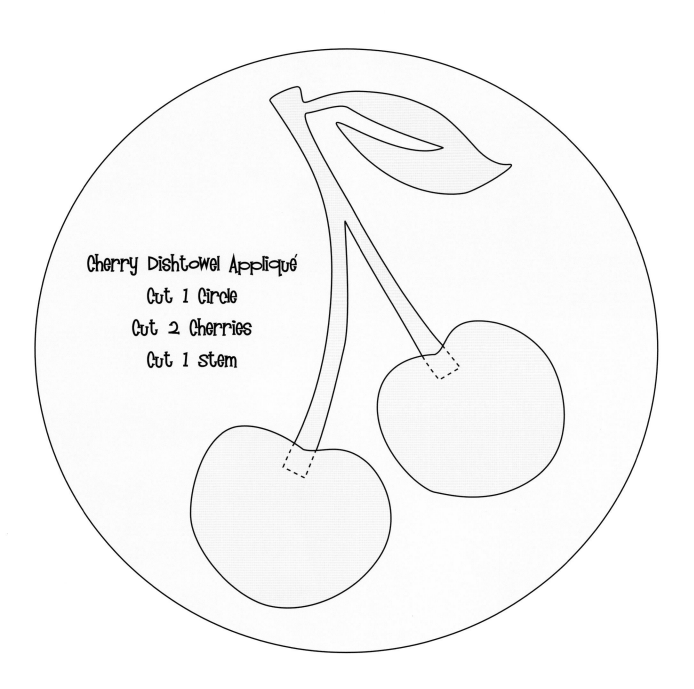

Cherry Dishtowel Appliqué

Cut 1 Circle

Cut 2 Cherries

Cut 1 stem

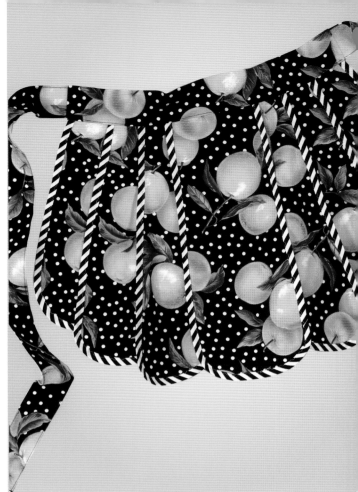

oranges

It's not often that one receives fabric that truly takes your breath away. That's exactly what this orange collection from Michael Miller Fabrics did for me. It was love at first cut. Paired up with striking black and white, which never goes out of style, this collection is simply stunning. Goodness, I feel like I could be right in the Orange Orchard making a commercial!

So pick the oranges right off the fruit tree and make up the entire collection.

Sun-Kissed Oranges Quilt

Finished size: 58" x 58"

Fabric Requirements

Fabric A 2 yards orange focal for block centers & inner border

Fabric B 7/8 yard white clip dot for block background & sashing

Fabric C 1 yard black & white stripe for frame & outer border

Fabric D 3/8 yard black w/ gray dots for block points

Fabric E 1/2 yard for binding

Backing 4 yards

Cutting Guide

Fabric A:
- Cut 4 squares 7-1/2" x 7-1/2"
- Cut 1 square 4" x 4"
- Cut 4 strips 10" x 64" on the length of grain

Fabric B:
- Cut 8 squares 5-1/2" x 5-1/2"
- Cut 16 squares 4-1/4" x 4-1/4"
- Cut 4 pieces 5" x 15"

Fabric C:
- Cut 4 strips 2" x WOF
  Sub cut 8 strips 2" x 7-1/2"
  8 strips 2" x 10-1/2"
- Cut 2 strips 1" x 4"
- Cut 2 strips 1" x 5"
- Cut 8 strips 3" x WOF

Fabric D:
- Cut 8 squares 5-1/2" x 5-1/2"

Fabric E:
- Cut strips 2-1/4" x WOF

Assembly

Block Points

1. Draw a line diagonally from corner to corner on the wrong side of the Fabric B 5-1/2" squares.

2. Place a Fabric B square on a 5-1/2" Fabric D square, RST. Stitch 1/4" on either side of the drawn line. Cut on the drawn line and press the half square triangles to the dark fabric. Trim each half-square triangle to a 4-3/4" square.

3. Cut the half-square triangles once more on the diagonal as shown to make block point units. Separate into 2 piles.

4. Sew a block point unit to one side of a 4-1/4" Fabric B square, matching the corner of the block point with the corner of square. Press the seam to the block point. Repeat with second block point to make one corner unit.

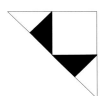

Make 32 units.

Center Blocks

1. Sew 2, 2" x 7-1/2" Fabric C block frame segments on opposite sides of a 7-1/2" Fabric A block center square. Press seam toward block frame. Sew 2, 2" x 10-1/2" segments to the remaining two sides of the block center. Press seams toward block frame.

2. Find the center of the frame block and match with the center of the previously made corner units. Pin and stitch, RST. Press seams toward center square.

Make 4, 15" x 15" blocks

Small Inner Block

1. Sew the 2, 1" x 4" Fabric C strips to opposite sides of the 4" Fabric A square. Press seams toward strips.

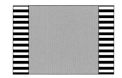

2. Sew the 2, 1" x 5" Fabric C strips to the remaining two side of the Fabric A square. Press seams toward strips.

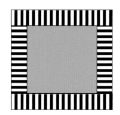

3. Add a 5" x 15" Fabric B sashing unit to either side of the inner block. Press seams toward sashing unit.

Assembly

1. Lay out two center blocks with a 5" x 15" Fabric B sashing strip in the middle. Sew the pieces RST to form a row. Press seams to outer edge. Make two rows.

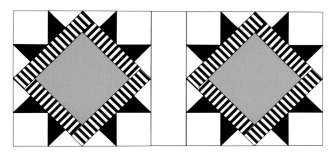

2. Lay out the two rows with the inner block/sashing unit in the middle, as shown.

3. Sew the rows, RST, to form the quilt center. Press seams toward sashing strip.

Mitered Borders

1. Join the 8, 3" x WOF Fabric C strips together in pairs to make 4, 3" x 64" outer border strips.

2. Sew the 4, 10" x 64" Fabric A inner border strips to the 4, 3" x 64" outer border strips, RST. Make 4 border pieces that measure 11-1/2" x 64".

3. Refer to General Instructions – Mitered Borders on page 10 to sew the border strips to the quilt center.

4. Refer to General Instructions – Backing and Assembling the Layers on page 11.

5. Quilt as desired.

6. Refer to General Instructions – Binding on page 11 to attach the binding to the quilt.

sun·kissed oranges quilt

oranges Table Runner

Finished size: 14-1/2" x 42"

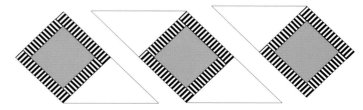

Fabric Requirements

Fabric A	1/4 yard orange focal for blocks
Fabric B	3/8 yard white clip dot for background
Fabric C	1/4 yard black & white stripe for block frame
Fabric D	1/4 yard black w/ gray dots for binding
Backing	20" x 48"

Cutting Guide

Fabric A:
• Cut 3 squares 7-1/2" x 7-1/2"

Fabric B:
• Cut 2 squares 11-1/4" x 11-1/4"
  Sub cut diagonally in half to
  make 4 triangles

Fabric C:
• Cut 3 strips 2" x WOF
  Sub cut 6 strips 2" x 7-1/2"
  6 strips 2" x 10-1/2"

Fabric D:
• Cut 3 strips 2-1/4" x WOF

Assembly

Blocks

1. Refer to Sun-kissed Oranges Quilt Center Block instructions, step 1, on page 59 to make 3 framed blocks. Do not add the block points.

2. Sew the Fabric B triangles to the center blocks as shown. Press seams toward block frame.

3. Join into rows.

4. Quilt as desired.

5. Trim the runner 1/4" beyond the outer point of the blocks.

6. Refer to General Instructions – Binding on page 11 to complete the table runner.

Oranges Table Runner

oranges Table Topper

Finished size: 25" x 25"

Sun-Kissed oranges cake

from the kitchen of my fabulous sister, Heidi Fisher

Cake:

1 package yellow cake mix

Orange juice
(use in place of water, same amount)

Oil and Eggs as listed on the box.

1 – 3 oz. box of Orange Gelatin,
divided in half

Make the cake as directed on the box,
mixing in the 1/4 cup of Orange Gelatin
powder with all of the other ingredients.

Place in 2 large bread pans or a 9 x 13 pan
which has been greased and floured. Bake
as directed and cool completely.

Remove from pans and frost.

Frosting:

1 tub of Cool Whip

8 oz. sour cream

3/4 cup sugar

1/4 cup orange gelatin powder
(about half of the 3 oz. box)

1/2 tsp. vanilla

Mix all ingredients together well and
refrigerate while the cake cools. If making a
9 x 13 pan, use half the amount of Cool Whip,
sour cream, sugar, and vanilla but the same
amount of gelatin powder. Enjoy!

Fabric Requirements

Fabric A   5/8 yard orange focal fabric for block center & border

Fabric B   1/2 yard stripe for block frame & binding

Fabric C   1/2 yard clip dot white for block background & corner squares

Fabric D   1/4 yard black & gray dot for block points

Fabric E   3/4 yard backing

Cutting Guide

Fabric A:
• Cut 1 square 7-1/2" x 7-1/2"
• Cut 4 pieces 6-1/2" x 15"

Fabric B:
Refer to General Instructions – Bias Binding on page 9 before cutting.
• Cut 1 strip 2" x WOF
   Sub cut 2 strips 2" x 7-1/2"
   2 strips 2" x 10-1/2"

Fabric C:
• Cut 4 squares 4-1/4" x 4-1/4"
• Cut 2 squares 5-1/2" x 5-1/2"
• Cut 4 squares 6-1/2" x 6-1/2"

Fabric D:
• Cut 2 squares 5-1/2" x 5-1/2"

Assembly

1. Make one block following instructions for block points and center blocks in Sun-kissed Oranges Quilt on page 59. Block will measure 15" x 15".

2. Sew 2, 6-1/2" x 15" Fabric A strips to opposite sides of block.

3. Sew a 6-1/2" x 6-1/2" Fabric C square to each end of the remaining 6-1/2" x 15" Fabric A strips.

4. Add strips to remaining sides of block.

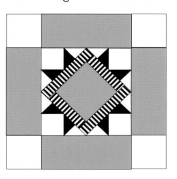

Scalloped Edge

Two Sisters Tip

*When marking any fabric it is always best to try out your marking pen or pencil on a scrap of fabric you are using. Hand wash the sample to ensure it will not be permanent on your project. This way you will know if this marker will work on your fabric & you won't be disappointed if the marks don't wash out. ***I like to mark scallops on the reverse side of the project and then I don't have to worry about marks coming out.*

1. When making a scalloped border the scallops are drawn on before quilting. This way when you or your quilter quilts the project, you will know where the border will end. This will also be the guideline for sewing on the binding.

2. Trace the border and corner scallops on pages 66-67 onto template plastic and cut out.

3. Use the border scallop template to mark scallops on the side borders of the table topper. Find the center of the block on each side and measure out 3-1/4" from the outer block seam line. Mark this point with a marker. Measure 1-3/8" from the outer edge of the border and mark this line across all outer edges. Draw 8 scallops using the border scallop template.

4. Using the corner scallop template, mark the 4 corners.

STOP: Do not cut on the marked line! You must complete quilting prior to cutting and binding your scallop edge.

Quilting

Quilt the top as desired.

Scalloped Binding

1. A bias binding is an absolute must for curved edges! A narrow single-fold bias binding is required. Make approximately 185" of bias binding. See bias binding instructions on page 9.

2. Using a 1" bias tape maker, follow manufacturer's instructions to make single fold bias tape.

Adding the Binding

1. Before binding, machine baste along the marked edge of the scalloped border. This will keep the edges from stretching or shifting as you sew on the binding. You can now trim a few inches away from the scalloped edge to eliminate bulk when sewing on the binding. On the inside of the scallops, clip and trim a small bit into the point allowing the quilt to stretch flat when the binding is sewn on.

2. Working on the front side of the quilt, position the binding on the quilt top with all raw edges even.

3. Leave a 10" tail before beginning to sew. This will ensure you have adequate binding to join on the curve. Using a walking foot is ideal for sewing the binding to the quilt. Open the binding and beginning in the center of a scallop sew, the binding to the quilt top catching only a single layer of fabric.

4. Sew using a 1/4" seam. Ease the binding around the curves. Stitch to the base of the V, stop with the needle down at that point. Lift the presser foot, pivot the quilt and binding to begin sewing out of the V. Put the presser foot down and sew out of the V, taking care not to stitch any pleats in the binding. Lift the presser foot and pivot the quilt and binding until the binding edge is again even with the marked line on the quilt. Lower the presser foot and continue stitching around the quilt. Join the binding ends to complete the binding.

5. Trim the excess batting and backing at the edge of the binding. Turn the binding to the back side of the quilt. Stitch down by hand. The binding will fold over itself at the inside corners like a reverse mitered corner.

6. Turn the binding to the back of the table topper and hand stitch in place.

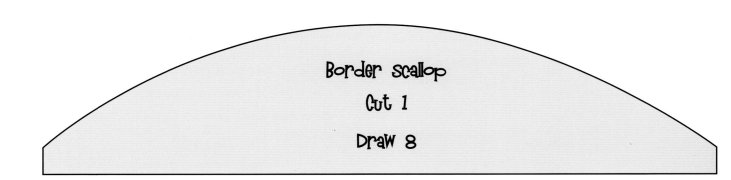

Border scallop

Cut 1

Draw 8

Corner scallop

Cut 1

Draw 4

Oranges Table Topper

oranges Apron

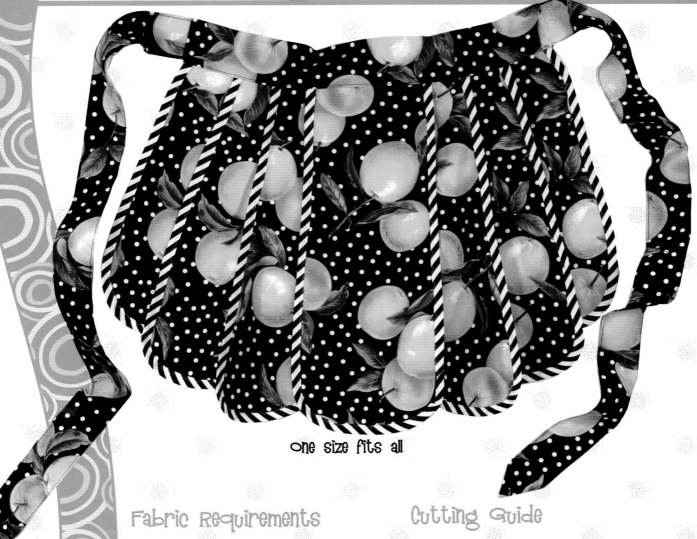

one size fits all

Fabric Requirements

Fabric A   3/4 yard orange focal

Fabric B   1/2 yard if making your own
binding OR
4-1/2 yards, 1/2 " double fold
pre-made binding

Cutting Guide

Trace the pattern pieces on pages 70-71. Lay
out the pieces on Fabric A following the straight
of grain arrows. Pin in place and cut out.

Fabric A:
- Cut 2 strips 2-3/4" x 35"
- Cut 1 strip 5-1/2" x 19"

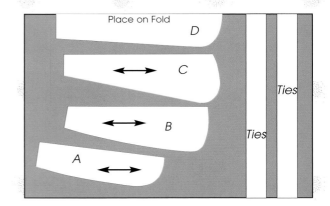

Assembly

Ties

1. Narrowly hem down both sides of the 2-3/4" x 35" Fabric A strips turning under all raw edges to make the apron ties.

2. Fold each tie in half RST. Stitch across one end of tie at an angle. Trim. Turn inside out. Using a tool, poke out corner. Center seam on back side of tie and press.

Apron Body

1. Refer to General Instructions – Bias Strips & Binding on page 9 to make your own bias binding.

2. Bind the 2 A pieces on the curved and side edge. Leave the straight edge at top raw.

3. Place an A piece on a B piece, wrong sides together and matching at point #1. Sew together. Repeat for opposite side of apron. Bind the edges as shown, leaving the straight edge at top raw.

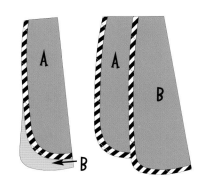

4. Place a B/A piece to a C piece, wrong sides together and matching at point #2. Sew together. Repeat for opposite side of apron and complete as in step #3.

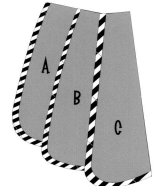

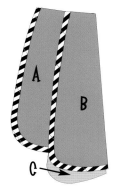

5. Place the C/B/A units on opposite sides of the D piece, wrong sides together and matching at point #3.

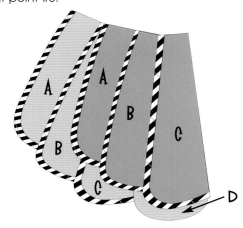

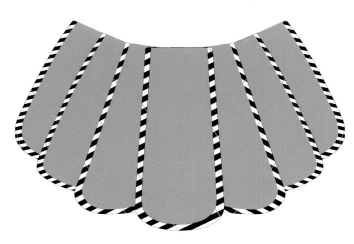

6. Sew binding to piece D leaving top edge raw.

Attaching Waistband

1. Press the 5-1/2" x 19" Fabric A strip in half, RST. Measure apron at top raw edge and cut the strip 1" longer to form the waistband.

2. Place the ties into each end of the waistband and sew down 1/4" on each side edge to 1/2" from lower edge. Turn inside out.

3. Pin raw edge of the waistband onto right side of the apron and stitch using a 1/2" seam allowance. Press waistband to inside folding under 1/2". Press seam to inside of band. Topstitch to finish apron.

Apron Patterns

①

Apron Piece A

Cut 2

Enlarge 140%

Straight of grain

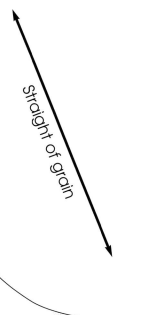

① ②

Straight of grain

Apron Piece B

Cut 2

Enlarge 140%

—— # 1

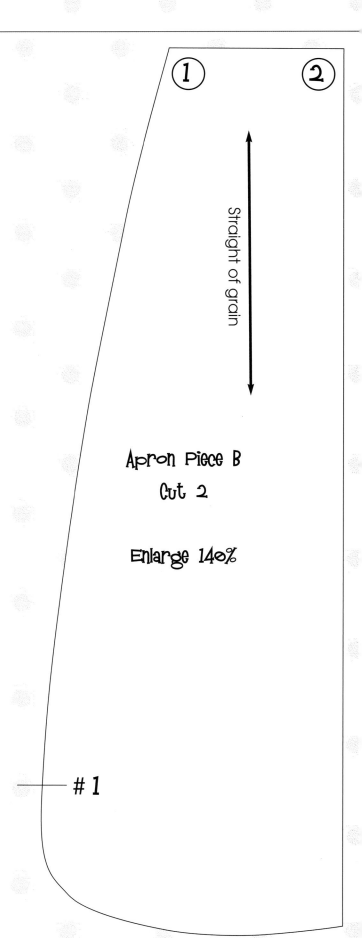

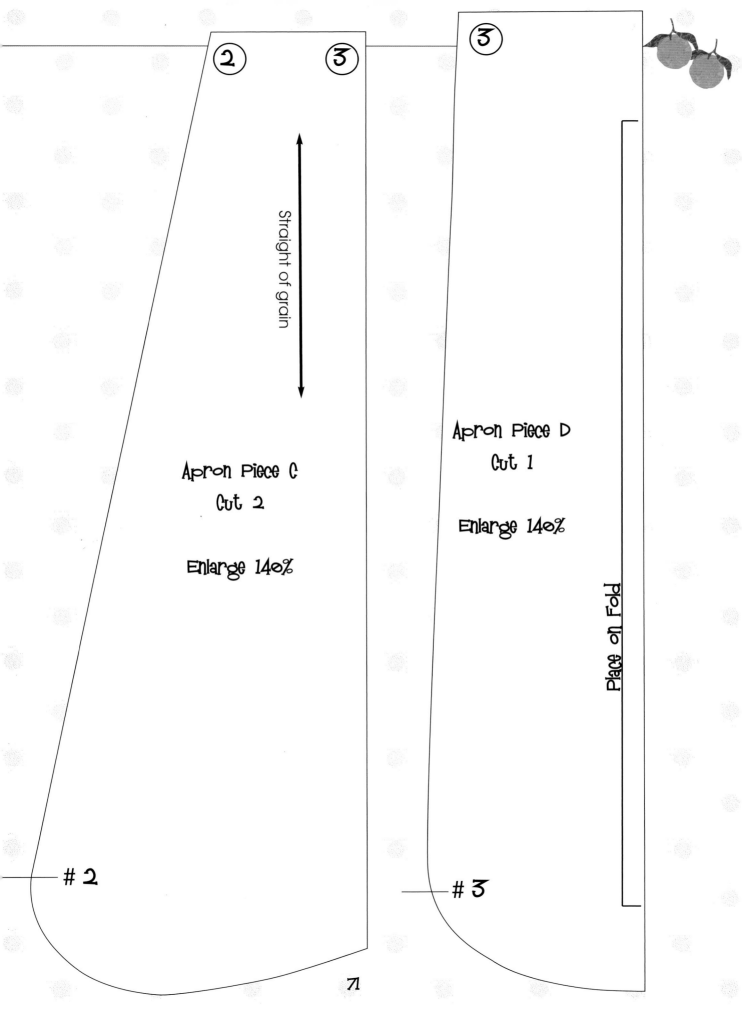

② ③

Straight of grain

Apron Piece C

Cut 2

Enlarge 140%

2

③

Apron Piece D

Cut 1

Enlarge 140%

Place on Fold

3

Finished size: 12" x 24"

oranges Wall Ar

Fabric Requirements

Fabric A   1/2 yard white & black print for background

Fabric B   8" x10" piece black dot for flower

Fabric C   3 fabrics, 1-1/2" x WOF strips for patchwork

Scraps   leaves & inner flower pieces

**1/2"
bias tape**   21"

Art Canvas   12" x 24" x 1"

Batting   17" x 30"

Cutting Guide

Fabric A:
- Cut 1 piece 13" x 34-1/2"
- Cut 1 piece 3-1/2" x 34-1/2"

Fabric B:
- Cut 1 flower using template on page 74

Fabric C:
- From each of the fabric strips
    Sub cut from 2 colors
    17 strips 1-1/2" x 2-1/2"
    Sub cut from 1 color
    1 strip 1-1/2" x 34-1/2"

Scraps:
- 1 inner flower—cut with pinking blade
- 2 A circles
- 2 B circles
- 1 C circle—center
- 1 D circle
- 1 A leaf
- 1 B leaf
- 1 C leaf

Assembly

1. Sew the 1-1/2" x 2-1/2" Fabric C pieces into 2 rows of 17 rectangles each, alternating colors.

2. Sew the 1-1/2" x 34-1/2" Fabric C strip in the center of the 2 strips to make one unit.

3. Trace the templates below and on page 74 onto fusible web. Refer to General Instructions - Appliqué on pages 8-9. Fuse the shapes to the fabric scraps and cut out. Fuse the cut out shapes to the 13" x 34-1/2" Fabric A background piece. Appliqué using method of choice.

4. Sew the 3" x 34-1/2" Fabric A piece and the appliquéd background piece to either side of the unit made in step 1.

5. Quilt as desired.

6. Stretch the quilted piece onto the 12" x 24" canvas being careful not to overstretch the project. Start on one side and using a staple gun, attach the long side with the patchwork onto the frame first. Repeat for opposite side. Finish by attaching the remaining ends. Fold the corners in and trim to eliminate bulk.

7. Trim and staple edges.

Wall Art Templates

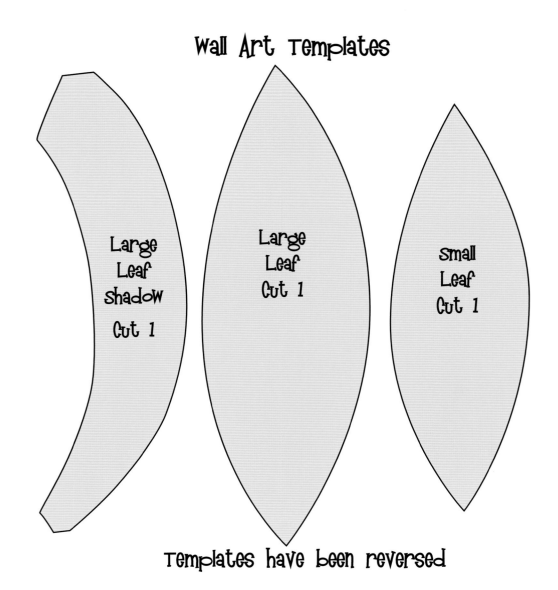

Large Leaf Shadow Cut 1

Large Leaf Cut 1

Small Leaf Cut 1

Templates have been reversed

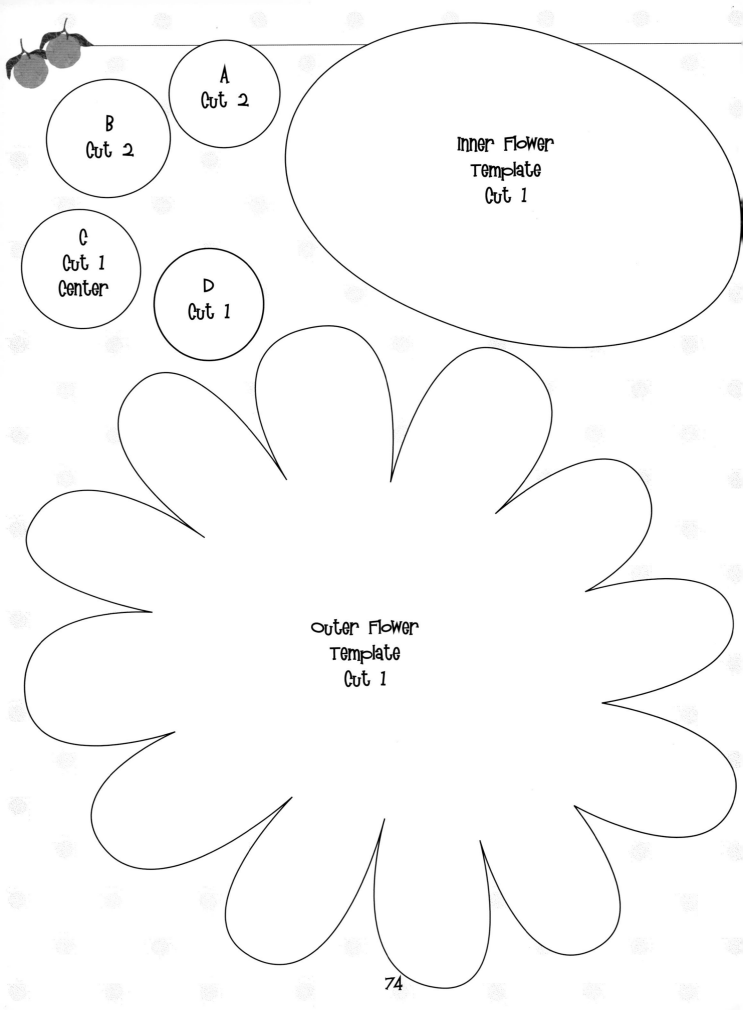

B
Cut 2

A
Cut 2

Inner Flower
Template
Cut 1

C
Cut 1
Center

D
Cut 1

Outer Flower
Template
Cut 1

74

oranges Dishtowel

Required ingredients:

Approximately 20" x 28" purchased dishtowel

Template for orange and leaf appliqués below

42" of 1/2" bias tape

Assembly

1. Refer to appliqué instructions on pages 8-9 before beginning.

2. Trace the orange and leaf templates below onto fusible web.

3. Measure 3-1/2" up from lower edge of the dishtowel. Center and fuse the orange and leaf shape in place. Appliqué using method of choice.

4. Measure 1" & 1-3/4" up from lower edge of dishtowel and mark lines. Run a basting stitch on these lines to use as a guide for placement. Stitch bias tape into place on both sides of the lines, turning under edges on reverse side.

Leaf Template
Cut 1

orange Template
Cut 1

Oranges Flower Cones

Required Ingredients

1 fat quarter for large or small cone, the outer and inner cone fabrics will be the same. If contrast is desired, purchase 2 fat quarters.

FAST 2 FUSE Heavyweight stiffener

3/8 yard Lightweight fusible one-sided interfacing

Two 1/4" eyelets (optional)

Assorted beads, buttons or trims as desired

Assembly

1. Cut 2, 10-1/2" squares from the fat quarter and 1, 10-1/2" square from the heavyweight stiffener. Layer stiffener between 10-1/2" squares and press together following manufacturer's instructions.

2. Place cone pattern from page 77 on square and cut out. Mark eyelet or buttonhole locations.

3. Satin stitch outside edge of cone.

4. Insert eyelets or make buttonholes at dots.

Ruffle

1. Cut one piece of lightweight interfacing and a fabric strip 2" x 30" (large cone) or 2" x 24" (small cone).

2. Iron interfacing onto the fabric strip. Using a rotary cutter with a pinking blade, cut each strip to measure 1-1/2" x 30" or 1-1/2" x 24".

3. Gather strip down the center to fit cone or to desired fullness. Sew to cone down the center of the gathered strip placing center at the top of cone. Shape into a cone and hand sew the edges closed down back side.

4. Cut a strip of fabric 1-1/2" x 22" (large cone) or 1-1/2" x 17" (small cone). Fold edges in 1/4" on both sides and press. Fold in half and stitch. Place strip through eyelet or buttonholes and tie knot at end for handle.

5. Embellish cone with beads, tassels, buttons, or trims as desired.

Oranges Flowers

1. Flowers can be made using 4-6 strips of fabric. The less fabric the more floppy the flowers.

2. Use the Clover® large Pom-Pom Maker and follow the manufacturer's instructions to make pom-poms in two sizes.

3. Cut strips of 1/2" and 3/4" strips of fabric. Mix the strips up or use widths consistently.

4. Use an 18-gauge floral covered wire and wrap it around the center of the flower. Twist to secure. With floral tape twist down the stem adding leaves if desired. Trim wire to fit into desired project.

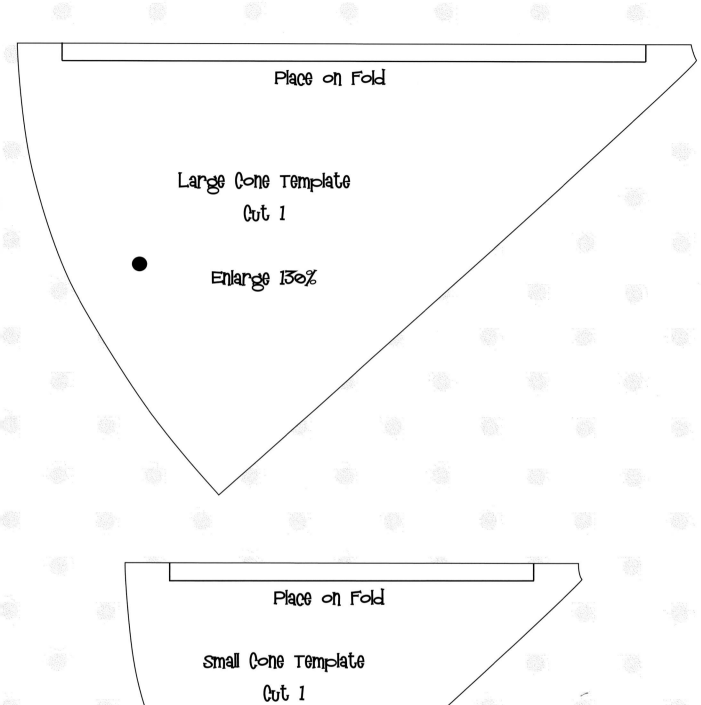

Place on Fold

Large Cone Template
Cut 1

Enlarge 130%

Place on Fold

Small Cone Template
Cut 1

Enlarge 130%

Apples

I often travel to Wenatchee, WA to
visit my son and his family.
Every spring it's a breathtaking drive over
the passes and into the valley.
Known as the apple capitol of the US
this area is abundant with many
varieties of fruit trees & each spring the hills
and valleys come alive with
white blossoms that dot the landscape.

Apples of every variety will become available as the
fall approaches and I grow eager in anticipation.
I am always amazed every year at
the small miracle that takes place from blossom
to beautiful fruit. The Apple Collection is a perfect
tribute to orchard stewards everywhere.

Apple Table Runner

Finished size: 30-1/2" x 17"

Fabric Requirements

Fabric A	1/4 yard solid cream for background
Fabric B	1/4 yard brown for outer triangles
Fabric C	1/8 yard green for border
Fabric D	1/2 yard backing
Fabric F	3, 6" x 6" squares in 3 colors for apple appliqués:
Scraps	3" x 3" for stems and leaves
Batting	1 piece 20" x 34"

Cutting Guide

Fabric A:
• Cut 3 squares 8-1/4" x 8-1/4"

Fabric B:
• Cut 4 squares 5-3/4" x 5-3/4"
  Subcut diagonally in half to make
  8 triangles

Fabric C:
• Cut 3 strips 1-1/2" x WOF
  Sub cut into:
  #1—6 strips 1-1/2" x 5-3/4"
  #2—2 strips 1-1/2" x 7-1/2"
  #3—2 strips 1-1/2" x 11-3/4"
  #4—2 strips 1-1/2" x 13"

Fabric D:
• Cut two pieces 18" x 20"

Fabric F: Appliqués
• Cut 3 Apples, stems and leaves
  from templates on page 83.

Refer to General Instructions - Appliqué
on pages 8-9.

Assembly of Apples Blocks

Two Sisters Tip

When machine appliquéing a small piece, such as the stem and leaves in this project, try using a small decorative stitch. A good one to try looks like a small lightning bolt on most machines and is a good way to have full coverage while not overpowering your design, like a buttonhole stitch might.

Using the appliqué method of choice, center and stitch the apples to the 3, 8-1/4" x 8-1/4" background squares. Complete by adding the stems and leaves. Trim to 3, 7-1/2" x 7-1/2" squares.

Assembly of Apple Runner

1. Gently pinch and press the 8 triangles in half to find the center. Repeat for the apple blocks. Stitch triangles to top and bottom edges of the apple blocks, matching at centers. Lay out apple blocks in color order of choice. Add a triangle to the left edge of the first block and right edge of the third block.

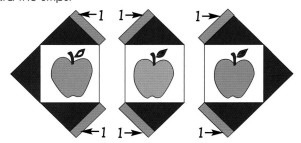

2. Add the 6, #1 strips as shown. Press seams toward the strips.

3. Add the 2, #2 strips as shown: Press seams toward the strips.

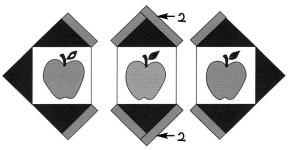

4. Add the 2, #3 strips as shown. Press seams toward the strips.

5. Add the 2, #4 strips as shown. Press seams toward the strips.

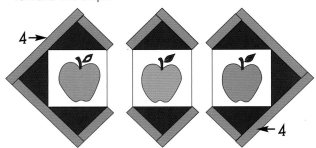

6. Sew the 3 apple sections RST, matching seams. Press seams open.

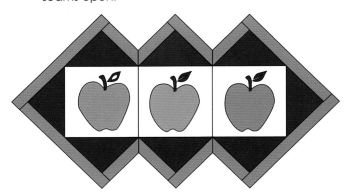

Backing

1. Stitch the 18" x 20" Fabric D pieces RST leaving a 6" opening in the center of seam. Press seam open.

2. Layer backing over batting, right side up.

3. Place apple runner top RST with backing. Stitch around all edges. Clip at corners and turn inside out. Use a corner tool to poke out corners. Press all edges and points. Slip stitch center closed.

4. Quilt as desired.

Cut 2
Closed Leaves

Cut 3
stems

Cut 1
open Leaf

Cut 3
Apples

Apple Baker's Apron

Fabric Requirements

Main fabric	12" x 21-1/2"
Pocket	13" x 21-1/2"
Waistband	2 pieces 5" x 44"
Apple	4" x 4"
Leaf and Stem	Scrap
Binding	1/8 yard

Assembly

1. Using the template on page 85, appliqué the apple on one side of the apron pocket, through one layer of fabric only.

2. Fold the apron pocket in half and press. Divide the pocket into 3 equal sections and mark with chalk or a quilter's pencil.

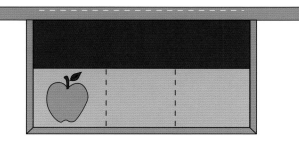

3. Match the lower raw edges of the apron and pocket. Stitch in place following the chalk lines to divide the large pocket into three smaller pockets. Baste at sides.

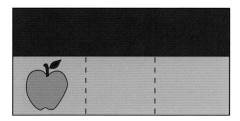

4. Refer to General Instructions - Binding on page 11 to make 45" of binding.

5. Sew binding around the sides and bottom of apron.

6. Sew the 2, 5" x 44" waistband pieces RST. Press seam open.

7. Fold the joined pieces in half and press under 1/4" on both sides.

8. Center the piece and sew RST to top of apron to form the waistband.

9. Fold in ends of waistband and stitch across the entire band closing the edges of the fold.

Cut 1 each of
Apple
stem
Leaf

Apple Dishtowel

Required ingredients:
- Approximately 20" x 28" purchased dishtowel
- Template on page 83 for apple appliqué
- 22" ribbon
- 22" of 5/8" rick rack trim
- 6" x 6" fabric square for apple
- Scraps for leaf and stem

Refer to General Instructions - Appliqué on pages 8-9.

1. Measure 3-3/4" up from lower edge of dishtowel. Center and fuse the apple, stem, and leaf in place. Appliqué using method of choice.

2. Measure 2-1/2" from lower edge of dishtowel and mark. Place top of ribbon on this mark and sew into place. Turn the ribbon edges under on the reverse side of dishtowel. Place rick rack trim at the top edge of the ribbon. Sew into place turning edges under on reverse side.

Apple Metro Market Bag

Fabric Requirements

Fabric A	3/8 yard green for body section
Fabric B	1/4 yard focal fabric for side/bottom panels
Fabric C	1/4 yard solid cream for pocket
Fabric D	1/4 yard brown for straps
Fabric E	6" x 6" blue for apple
Scrap	leaves & stem
Lining	5/8 yard for body section, side/bottom panels

Heavyweight interfacing
1 yard for body section, side/bottom panels

Plastic rectangle for bottom of bag

Cutting Guide

Fabric A:
• Cut 2 pieces 12-1/2" x 14-1/2"

Fabric B:
• Cut 1 piece 8" x 41-1/2"

Fabric C:
• Cut 1 piece 7-1/2" x 15"

Fabric D:
• Cut 2 pieces 3" x 42"

Lining & Interfacing:
• Cut 2 pieces 12-1/2" x 13-1/2"
• Cut 1 piece 8" x 40-1/2"

Refer to General Instructions - Appliqué on pages 8-9.

Appliqué

1. Fold the 7-1/2" x 15" Fabric C piece in half to form the pocket. Use the templates below to cut out the apple, stem, and leaf appliqués. Center the apple shapes onto one side of pocket and fuse in place. Appliqué in place through a single layer of fabric.

2. Press the top edge of each Fabric A body section under 1/4". Fold and press under another 1" to create a clean finish on the body's top edge.

3. Center pocket onto one body section, matching raw edges at bottom. Baste at sides and lower edge.

straps

1. Turn the long edges of the Fabric B straps under 1/4" and press. Fold the straps in half and press well.

2. Measure 12-1/2" in from the short ends of each strap. Stitch four or more lines onto strap between these two points to reinforce handle area and to add aesthetic value.

←—12-1/2"—→   ←—12-1/2"—→

3. Place strap onto front body section covering 3/8" at the left edge of the pocket.

4. Pin in place and loop strap over top continuing down the pocket's right side edge. Topstitch in place starting from bottom edge of strap up to 1" below the body section fold line.

5. Reinforce the straps at the top of each strap at fold line at top of bag. Stitch the handle portion of the strap to give extra strength.

6. Repeat for second body unit.

Assembly of Bag and Lining

1. Press the top edge of the 8" x 4-1/2" Fabric B piece under 1/4". Fold and press under another 1" to create a clean edge on the side/bottom panels.

2. Pin the body sections and the side panel RST, easing in to fit. Stitch, rounding the corners at the bottom of the bag. Repeat for lining. Clip corners.

3. Place the lining inside the outer bag with wrong sides together. Slip the lining's top edge under the 1" fold at the top of the bag.

4. Stitch around the top edge of the bag to finish.

5. Cut a piece of plastic to size and place in the bottom of the bag to add stability and support. If you prefer cut a piece of foam board and cover it with fabric.

Cut 1 each of Template
Apple
Stem
Leaf

Apple Place Mats & Napkins

Finished place mat size: 19-3/4" x 14-1/2"
Finished napkin size: 17-3/4" x 17-3/4"

Apple & Blackberry Crumble

from the kitchen of my dear friend, Linda Cunningham

Ingredients

6 Granny Smith apples (peeled, cored and cut in chunks)

2 lbs blackberries

1 cup sugar (more needed if fruit is tart)

1 tsp cinnamon

Tapioca for thickening

Place apples, sugar, cinnamon in a large pan, stirring until sugar is dissolved and apples start to soften. Add blackberries; stir gently as to not break up the berries. You should have juice from the fruit. Add as much tapioca as needed to lightly thicken the mixture. Pour mixture into a baking dish sprayed with cooking spray. Cover top with Topping and bake at 350 degrees until top is golden brown and the fruit is bubbly. Serve with ice cream or heavy cream poured over the top.

Topping

2 cups flour

1 cup sugar

1 cup cold butter (cut into cubes)

Mix flour and sugar. Cut in cold butter cubes with a pastry cutter or two table knives until mixture resembles small peas. Cover the top of crumble with topping.

Apple Place Mats
Makes 1 place mat

Fabric Requirements

Fabric A 3/4 yard apple focal
for front and back of mat

Fabric B 1/8 yard blue for accent color #1

Fabric C 1/8 yard green for accent color #2

Fabric D 1/4 yard brown circle print for binding

Batting 16" x 24"

Cutting Guide

Fabric A
- Cut 1 piece 10" x 15"
- Cut 1 piece 3-1/4" x 10"
- Cut 1 piece 3" x 3-1/4"
- Cut 1 piece 3" x 15"
- Cut 1 piece16" x 24"

Fabric B
- Cut 1 piece 2-1/2" x 3-1/4"
- Cut 1 piece 2-1/2" x 15"

Fabric C
- Cut 1 piece 2-1/2" x 14-1/2"

Fabric D
- Cut 2 pieces 2-1/4" x WOF

Assembly

1. Lay out Fabric A and Fabric B pieces as shown.

2. Sew Fabric A and Fabric B pieces RST. Press seams to darker color.

3. Join the two sections of the place mat together with Fabric C piece. Press seams to darker color.

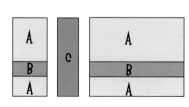

4. Lay back of place mat right side down. Place batting on top and finish with place mat top right side up.

5. Smooth out and pin at sides. Baste on outer edges. Press well. Quilt as desired or stitch in the ditch.

6. Trim mat to 19-1/2" x 14-1/4"

7. Refer to General Instructions - Binding on page 11 to attach binding.

Apple Napkins
Makes 2 napkins

Fabric Requirements

Fabric A: Blue print
- Cut 1 piece 20-1/2" x 20-1/2"

Fabric B: Brown circle print
- Cut 1 piece 20-1/2" x 20-1/2"

Focal Fabric: Cut 2 pieces 18-1/2" x 18-1/2"

Assembly

1. Place Fabric A and Fabric B RST.

2. On the wrong side of one fabric square draw a diagonal line from corner to corner. Mark a 1/4" sewing line on either side of the center line.

3. With Fabric A still on top of Fabric B, stitch along marked sewing lines.

4. Cut on the center line, between rows of stitching, to make 2 half square triangle units. Press seam allowances toward darker fabrics.

5. Pair up the units RST with opposite fabrics matching each other. Draw a line from corner to corner. Add 1/4" lines on both sides of drawn line and stitch along both lines.

6. Cut on the center line to create 2 hourglass units. Set seam, then press seam allowances to one side.

7. Square up each unit to 18-1/2" x 18-1/2" making certain to center the block at the 9-1/4" line.

8. Place one hourglass unit RST with focal fabric square. Stitch around napkin leaving a 3" opening for turning. Trim seams to 1/4" clipping at corners. Press. Stitch 1/4" around napkin edge closing seam as you go. For stability stitch an X in the center of the napkin.

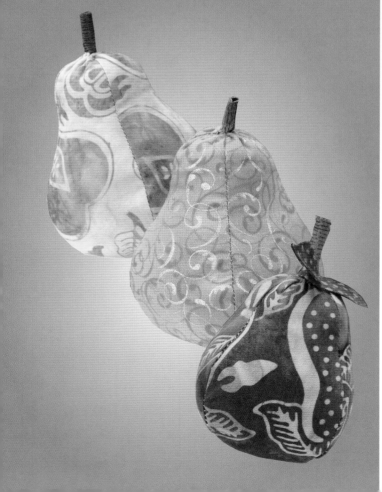

Pears

I always loved the holidays when I was growing up. My mother would make Christmas simply wonderful—turning our home into a vision of Sugarplums by the time this holiday rolled around. It was a family event to decorate the tree. Each piece of tinsel was hung separately. I can remember groaning as I thought about the week it would take to carefully place each piece on our always-enormous tree!

My sassy Pear Partridge with coordinating accessories will fit right into this festive occasion, adding to your holiday table and helping to make your season simply delightful!

Pear Christmas Wall Hanging

Finished size: approximately 41-1/2" x 41-1/2"

Fabric Requirements

Fabric A   3/4 yard red for pinwheels & berries

Fabric B   1 yard green for pear, wreath, pinwheel, leaves, border, & binding

Fabric C   5/8 yard light green for pinwheel & inner wreath background

Fabric D   3/4 yard cream for background

Fabric E   6" x 6" square gold for bird

Fabric F   6" x 10" rectangle for tree branch

Fabric G   4" x 4" square gold accent for bird

Backing   1-1/4 yard
Note: If your quilt will be quilted on a longarm machine, purchase 2-1/2 yards of backing fabric

Batting   45" x 45" piece

Cutting Guide

Fabric A:
- Cut 6 strips 2-3/4" x WOF
  Sub cut into 48 rectangles 2-3/4" x 5"
- Cut assorted small circles for berry embellishment on wreath
- Cut 2 strips 2" x 38-1/2"
- Cut 2 strips 2" x 41-1/2"

Fabric B:
- Cut 1 strip 5" x WOF
  Sub cut into 4 rectangles 5" x 9-1/2"
- Cut 1 strip 6" x WOF
  Sub cut into 2 squares 6" x 6"
- Cut 4 strips 2-3/4" x WOF
  Sub cut into 48 squares 2-3/4" x 2-3/4"
- Cut 4 squares 2-1/2"
- Cut 4 strips 2" x WOF
- Cut 4 strips 2-1/4" x WOF for binding

Fabric C:
- Cut one square 9-1/2" x 9-1/2"
- Cut 4 strips 2-3/4" x WOF
  Sub cut into 48 squares 2-3/4" x 2-3/4"

Fabric D:
- Cut 2 squares 6" x 6"
- Cut 6 strips 2-3/4" x WOF
  Sub cut into 48 rectangles 2-3/4" x 5"

Refer to General Instructions – Appliqué on pages 8-9.

Pinwheel Block Assembly

1. Draw a diagonal line, corner to corner, on the wrong side of the 2-3/4" Fabric B and Fabric C squares. Mark an additional line 1/2" from the drawn diagonal line to make a bonus half-square triangle**.

2. Place the marked Fabric B square on the 2-1/2" x 5" Fabric A rectangle, RST and aligning raw edges. Stitch on the two drawn lines. Trim 1/4" from each sewn line. Press seams open.

Bonus half-square triangle

3. Repeat process for the 2-3/4" Fabric C square, on the opposite end of the Fabric A rectangle. Check the direction of your stitching line before sewing.

Bonus half-square triangle

4. Make a total of 48 rectangle units.

** The basket and dishtowel in this collection will utilize the bonus half-square triangles!

5. Sew the 2-3/4" x 5" Fabric D rectangles to the left side of a pieced rectangle unit to make each pinwheel unit. The rectangles will be reversed in half the pinwheel units giving two colors of pinwheel centers. Make 48 pinwheel units

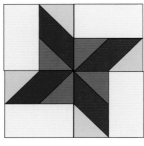 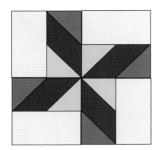

Make 24 A units   *Make 24 B units*

6. Join 4 pinwheel units to form a block. Make 6 blocks of unit A and 6 blocks of unit B. Blocks will finish 10" x 10".

Make 6   *Make 6*

Wreath

1. Draw a diagonal line from corner to corner on the 2, 6" Fabric D squares. Place a Fabric D square on top of a 6" Fabric B square, RST and aligning fabric. Sew 1/4" on either side of the drawn line. Cut into 2 pieces. Press seam to dark color and trim half-square triangle to 5" x 5".

Make 4 corner units

2. Sew the corner units to either side of a 5" x 9-1/2" Fabric B rectangle. Press seam toward center unit.

Make 2

Wreath Center

1. Draw a diagonal line from corner to corner on the wrong side of the 2-1/2" Fabric B squares. Place a Fabric B square at the corners of the 9-1/2" x 9-1/2" Fabric C square, RST. Sew on the drawn lines. Trim away excess fabric to 1/2". Press seam to outer edge.

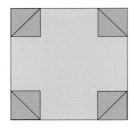 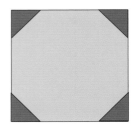

2. Sew the remaining Fabric B 5" x 9-1/2" rectangles to either side of the wreath center. Press seam to outer edge.

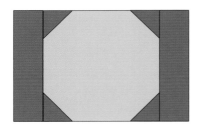

3. Cut out the branch, leaves, and bird using the templates on page 96. Refer to General Instructions - Appliqué on pages 8-9. Fuse the shapes to the wreath center and appliqué in place.

Berry Embellishment for Wreath & Bird

1. The Fabric A berries are very small. To attach them to the quilt top I use Liquid Stitch® and an applicator bottle with a small size tip. Pour some of the glue into the small applicator bottle.

2. Starch the fabric piece to be used for the berries several times until it is stiff. Refer to General Instructions – Starch on page 7. The stiffer the fabric the easier it will be to cut true circles. I prefer to free hand cut my circle for the berries. Remember there are no two berries alike, so you don't have to make them perfect. Free hand cutting allows for less stress. For the bird, template circles are provided on page 96 if you desire.

3. Lay out the wreath block rows as shown. Stitch the rows together matching seams. Press seams.

Assembly of Wall Hanging Top
Rows 1 & 3

1. Lay out the quilt top on a flat surface to make certain the pinwheel blocks alternate in color. Join 4 pinwheel blocks to make row one. Press seams toward center on both outer pinwheels blocks. Repeat for row 3.

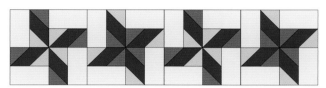

2. Sew 2 pinwheel blocks together. Repeat for the remaining 2 pinwheel blocks. Sew a pinwheel block section to either side of the center wreath. Press seams toward outer edges. Sew pinwheel rows 1 and 3 to the top and bottom edge of the center row.

3. Refer to General Instructions – Borders on pages 10-11 to add the 2" x WOF Fabric B border strips to the wall hanging center.

4. Refer to General Instructions – Backing and Assembling the Layers on page 11.

5. Quilt as desired.

Binding

Use the 2-1/4" x WOF Fabric B strips to bind the wall hanging. Refer to General Instructions – Binding on page 11 to bind and complete the wall hanging.

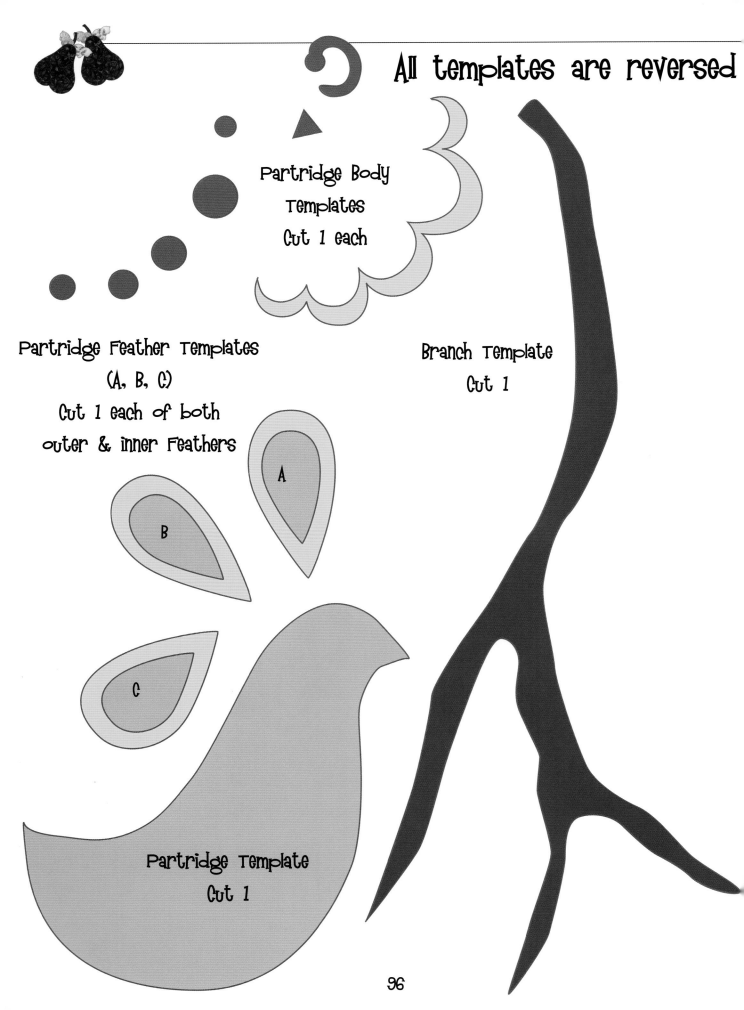

Partridge Body
Templates
Cut 1 each

Partridge Feather Templates
(A, B, C)
Cut 1 each of both
outer & inner feathers

Branch Template
Cut 1

A

B

C

Partridge Template
Cut 1

Pear Christmas Wall Hanging

Pear Table Runner

Finished size: 13" x 38"

Fabric Requirements

Fabric A   5" x 30" red dot for inner peppermints

Fabric B   1-5/8 yard green print for wreath units, border, binding, & backing

Fabric C   5" x 25" cream for inner peppermints

Batting   24" x 46"

Cutting Guide

Fabric A:
• Cut 6 squares 4-3/4" x 4-3/4"

Fabric B:
• Cut 4 strips 3-1/2" x WOF
    Sub cut 12 rectangles 3-1/2" x 7-1/2"
    Sub cut 12 squares 3-1/2" x 3-1/2"
• Cut 1 strip 2-3/4" x WOF
    Sub cut into 12 squares 2-3/4" x 2-3/4"
• Cut 2 pieces 23" x 23"

Fabric C:
    Cut 6 squares 4-3/4" x 4-3/4"

scrumptious Gingerbread Pear Cake

from the kitchen of my sweet friend, Sue Kitchel

Ingredients

1 purchased box gingerbread cake mix

1 can of Bartlett Pears – drained

Make cake according to box directions.
Cut up pears into small pieces and fold into cake batter.
Bake according to directions.

Caramel Sauce

1/4 cup butter

1 cup brown sugar

3 T cornstarch

1 cup cold water

2 tsp vanilla

Mix all ingredients and bring to a boil.
Serve cake warm with hot caramel sauce topped with fresh whipped cream. This is the most heavenly dessert!

Inner Peppermints

1. Draw a diagonal line from corner to corner on the wrong side of the 4-3/4" Fabric C squares.

2. Place the Fabric C squares on the 4-3/4" Fabric A squares, RST and aligning the edges. Sew 1/4" on either side of the drawn line. Cut on the center line to make 2 half-square triangles. Press seam to the darker color and trim to 4" x 4".

Make 12

3. Join 4 units to make one pinwheel square nesting seams. Refer to General Instructions – Nesting Seams on page 8. Make a total of 3 pinwheel squares.

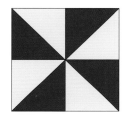

Make 3

4. Draw a diagonal line from corner to corner on the wrong side of the 2-3/4" Fabric B squares. Place a Fabric B square at the corners of each pinwheel square, RST. Sew on the drawn lines. Trim off excess fabric to 1/4" and press to outer edge. Make a total of 3 blocks.

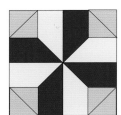

Make 3

Wreath Outer Units

1. Sew 1, 3-1/2" Fabric B square to each side of the 3-1/2" x 7-1/2" Fabric B rectangles. Press seams to center. Make 6 outer wreath units.

Make 6

2. Sew a 3-1/2" x 7-1/2" Fabric B rectangle to opposite edges of the 3 pinwheel blocks. Press seams to outer edge.

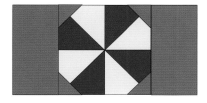

3. Make a pinwheel wreath block by sewing an outer wreath unit to the top and bottom of a pinwheel block.

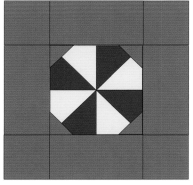

4. Use a ruler to draw a line from corner to corner on each of the 12 corners on the 3 pinwheel blocks. Stay stitch on this line to prevent stretching and then cut off corners just outside the sewn line.

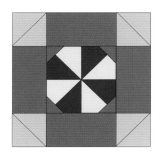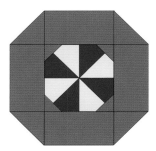

5. Join the 3 blocks together, referring to the photograph below. Press seams open.

Quilting

Quilt runner as desired to a muslin base. This is done since the runner will be finished with a backing instead of binding.

Finishing

1. To enclose the runner sew the 2, 23" Fabric B pieces RST, on the short edge, leaving a 4" opening in center of seam. Open and press.

2. Lay batting on a flat surface. Place the wrong side of the runner on the batting. Place the backing, RST, on runner. Pin well, smoothing out all wrinkles. Sew around raw edges using a 1/4" seam. Trim batting and excess fabric clipping inner V points. Reach through 4" opening in backing and pull the layers through to turn right side out. Use a tool for poking out corners. Press well, slipstitch the opening closed. If desired, stitch in the ditch around the peppermint to hold backing down.

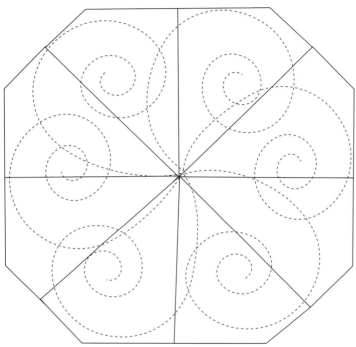

Quilting Suggestion

Pear Table Runner

Pear Dishtowel

Required Ingredients:

Approximately 20" x 28" purchased dishtowel

Template for pear appliqué below

7 half-square triangles trimmed to 1-1/2" x 1-1/2"
Refer to Pear Basket – Half-Square Triangles instructions on page 103 to make half-square triangles or use bonus half-square triangles from the Pear Christmas Wall Hanging.

Refer to General Instructions – Appliqué on pages 8-9.

Trace the pear template below onto fusible web.

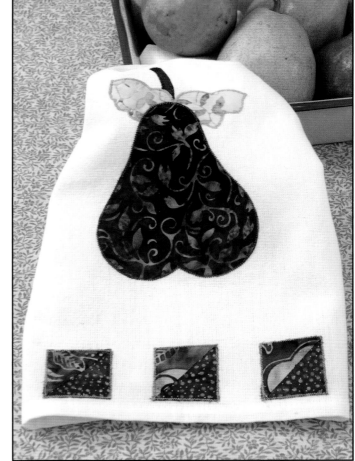

1. Measure 4" up from the lower edge of the dishtowel and mark. Center the bottom edge of the pear at this mark and place leaves and stem behind the pear. Fuse into place. Appliqué using method of choice.

2. Iron fusible web to the back of the half-square triangles. Fuse squares into place 1/2" from the bottom edge of the dishtowel and spaced 1" apart. Appliqué using method of choice.

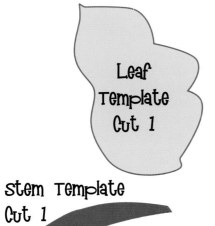

Leaf Template Cut 1

Stem Template Cut 1

Leaf Template Cut 1

Pear Template Cut 1

Pear Basket

Fabric Requirements

Note: if the Pear Christmas Wall Hanging was made, you will not have to make the half-square triangles. Trim the extra ones made in the pear quilt to 1-3/4" x 1-3/4". You will need 22 light green and 22 dark green.

Fabric A	1/4 yard red for half-square triangles
Fabric B	5/8 yard dark green for half-square triangles, lining, & handles
Fabric C	1/2 yard light green for half-square triangles & outer basket
Fusible Fleece	16" x 17"
Batting	2 pieces 2" x 12"

Cutting Guide

Fabric A:
- Cut 2 strips 2-1/2" x WOF
  Sub cut into 22 squares 2-1/2" x 2-1/2"
- Cut 2 strips 2-1/4" x 12"

Fabric B:
- Cut 1 strip 2-1/2" x WOF
  Sub cut into 11 squares 2-1/2" x 2-1/2"
- Cut 2 pieces 2-1/4" x 12"
- Cut 1 piece 14" x 21"

Fabric C:
- Cut 1 strip 2-1/2" x WOF
  Sub cut into 11 squares 2-1/2" x 2-1/2"
- Cut 1 piece 14-1/4" x 15-1/2"

Half-Square Triangles

1. Place a 2-1/2" Fabric A square and a 2-1/2" Fabric B square RST. Draw a diagonal line from corner to corner on the wrong side of one of the squares. Sew 1/4" on either side of drawn line. Cut on the drawn line to make 2 half-square triangles. Press seam to dark fabric. Trim to 1-3/4".

Make 22 A/B

2. Repeat step 1 with remaining 2-1/2" Fabric A squares and 2-1/2" Fabric C squares.

Make 22 A/C

Assembly

1. Sew 4 strips of 11 half-square triangles together, alternating colors.

Make 4

2. Sew 2 strips together, offsetting colors. Make 2 strip sets.

Make 2

3. Sew a strip set to opposite sides of the 14-1/4" x 15-1/2" Fabric C rectangle.

4. Press the fusible fleece to the wrong side of the rectangle/strip sets.

5. Quilt basket as desired.

6. Fold rectangle in half, RST. Sew the side seams of the basket matching seams in the strip sets.

Squarely Boxing the Corners

1. To box the bottom of the basket, work with the basket inside out. With the bag in an upright position, align the sewn side seam with the center bottom of the bag. Make sure the seam is truly centered by measuring with a ruler.

2. Measure 3-1/2" from the point. Draw a straight line across bottom at this measurement and pin in place. Make sure the fabric on the left and right side of seam are the same measurement. Sew on line. Trim seam to 1/4" and overcast edges. Repeat for other basket corner.

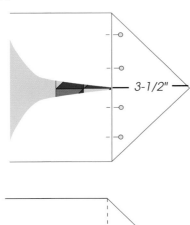

3-1/2"

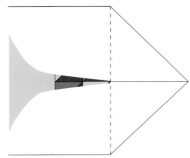

Handles

1. Press under 1/4" on one side of each 2-1/4" x 12" Fabric A and B strip. Place the two strips, RST. Lay a 2" x 12" batting piece on top, tucking it under 1/4" pressed fold. Sew layers together along unpressed edge. Open and press.

2. Fold length of handle in half, right side out. Measure in 2-1/2" from each end and mark with fabric marker.

3. Sew a decorative or zigzag stitch from the 2-1/2" mark to handle ends.

4. Fold handle in half and stitch from one end to the other end of handle, stopping at the 2-1/2" mark.

5. Measure 1-1/2" from each edge of basket and mark. Place the handle end at this mark and baste to basket.

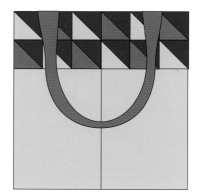

6. Repeat steps 1 - 5 for second handle.

Lining

1. Fold lining Fabric B, 14" x 21", RST, in half. Stitch side seams together.

2. Follow the Squarely Boxing the Corners instructions on page 103 to form lining corners.

3. Place the lining, wrong side down, into the basket. The lining and bag are now wrong sides together. Pin around top edge, catching handles into seam, and matching basket and lining side seams. Stitch. Clip seam. Pull lining out of basket 1/2" around top edge. Fold over to outside of basket edge to make a self binding. Stitch a seam to secure.

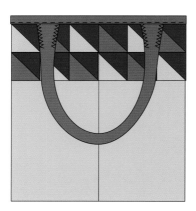

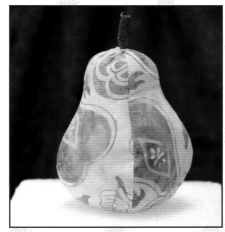

Christmas Pears

Small and Large

Use a scant 1/4" seam for all pears

Fabric Requirements:

Small pear
4 rectangles 2-3/4" x 4-1/4"

Leaf for small pear
1-3/4" x 4" piece
1-3/4" x 2" piece fusible web

Large pear
4 rectangles 3-1/4" x 6"

Leaf for large pear (optional)
2-1/4" x 6" piece
2-1/4" x 3 piece fusible web

Stem for small or large pear
1-1/4" x 1-1/2" piece

1. Trace the templates on page 107 and transfer to the wrong side of a pear rectangle fabric piece. Pin or baste the 4 rectangle fabric pieces together with the marked rectangle on top. Cut out the 4 pear sections at one time. A small rotary blade works well for this project.

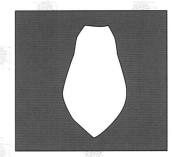

2. Pin 2 cut out pear sections RST and sew, backstitching at the top and bottom of the pear stopping at the dot. Sew the remaining 2 pieces together. Place the 2 sections RST and join, sewing around the entire pear. Clip curves and turn pear right side out.

3. Fill the bottom of the small pear with a small amount of short grain rice, crushed walnuts, or pellets. This will add weight and stabilize the bottom of the pear so it won't tip easily. Stuff the remaining part of the pear with polyester stuffing,

4. Stuff the entire large pear with rice, walnuts, or pellets. You will need to lightly pound the pear up and down as you fill the pear to distribute the filler evenly. Finish in the same manner as the small pear. The leaf on the large pear is optional.

stem & Leaves for small and large pears

Two Sisters Tip

Using freezer paper to make a small template is an effective way to get an accurate cut. The paper is flexible and makes cutting easier and more precise. Iron the freezer paper directly onto the fabric and cut out the shape. A freezer paper template can be used many times.

stem

1. Spread a fair amount of Liquid Stitch® glue over the entire stem piece. Gently roll the stem into a tight cylinder. Let dry completely.

2. Hand sew a basting stitch around the edge of the top of pear turning under 1/4". Place the stem in the center of the open space and stuff into filler. Gently pull the basting stitches tight. Sew several secure stitches back and forth through stem and pear. Trim stem if necessary for height proportion and to make a clean cut.

Leaves

1. Starch fabric before fusing following General Instructions - Starch on page 7. To make one leaf, iron the fusible web onto half of the 1-3/4" x 4" leaf fabric. Remove the paper and press the remaining side of fabric onto the fused section to make one fused fabric piece. Trace the template on page 107 onto freezer paper and cut out the leaf shape. Iron shape onto the fused material and cut out the leaf.

2. Wrap the leaf around the pear stem. Place a small dot of Liquid Stitch® on top of one leaf and criss-cross the second leaf over the top it. Let dry. To make ornament, add gold beading for hanger by stitching to base at stem of pear.

Leaf Template

Cut 1

Leaf Template

Cut 1

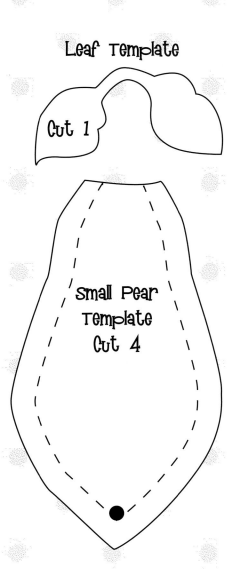

Small Pear
Template
Cut 4

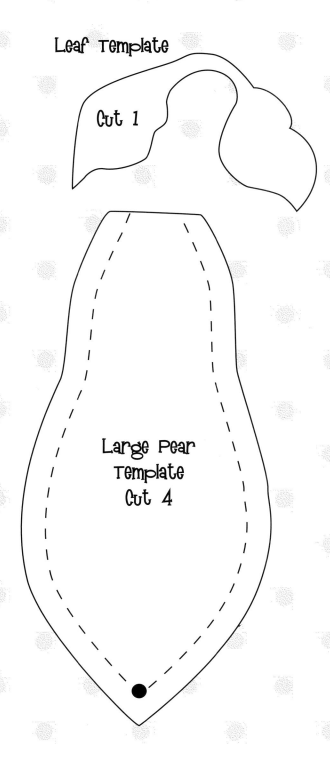

Large Pear
Template
Cut 4

Peppermint
Place Mats & Napkins

Finished place mat size: 14" x 14"
Finished napkin size: 16-1/4" x 16-1/4"

Peppermint Place Mats

Makes 2 place mats

Fabric Requirements

Fabric A	1/4 yard red
Fabric B	1/4 yard cream
Fabric C	1/2 yard for backing
Batting	1/2 yard

Cutting Guide

For 1 place mat:

Fabric A:
• Cut 2 squares 8-1/2" x 8-1/2"

Fabric B:
• Cut 2 squares 8-1/2" x 8-1/2"

Fabric C:
• Cut 2 pieces 9" x 18"

Assembly

1. Draw a diagonal line, corner to corner, on the wrong side of the 2, 8-1/2" x 8-1/2" Fabric B squares. Place a Fabric B square on top of a 8-1/2" x 8-1/2" Fabric A square, RST. Sew 1/4" on either side of the drawn line. Cut on the drawn line to make 2 half-square triangles.

2. Press to the dark fabric and trim to 7-3/4" x 7-3/4".

3. Repeat for the second pair of 8-1/2" squares.

4. Lay out the 4 half-square triangles as shown to make one pinwheel block.

5. Measure 2-1/2" in at the corners of each place mat edge and mark. Draw a straight line across and cut off the corners.

6. To enclose the place mat sew the 2, 9" x 18" Fabric C pieces RST and make a center seam leaving a 4" opening.

7. Lay batting on a flat surface. Lay the place mat backing and front RST on the batting. Pin well, smoothing out all wrinkles. Sew around all raw edges of place mat using a 1/4" seam.

8. Trim batting and excess fabric. Make a small slice in the batting down the center. Reach in and pull the place mat through both layers to turn inside out. Use a tool for poking out corners. Press well, slipstitch the opening closed. If desired stitch in the ditch around the place mat to hold the backing down or refer to the quilting suggestion on page 100 to quilt the center of the place mat.

Napkins

Fabric Requirements

14" x 14" square of pear focal

20" x 20" square of red

1. On the wrong side of both fabric squares mark the edges at the center point. With RST and center marks matching lay the 14" x 14" square on the 20" x 20" square.

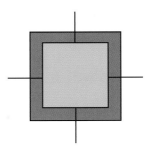

2. Pin the raw edges of the fabric squares RST. Begin pinning at the center marks and work out to the corners, placing a pin 1/4" from each corner of the 14" x 14" square. The 20" x 20" square will be 'bunched up' in the center to allow for the pinning of the raw edges.

3. Sew the top and bottom edges of the squares starting and stopping at the 1/4" corner pin.

4. Repeat to sew the remaining 2 sides. Leave a 3" opening on one side.

Note: The 20" x 20" square will form 'flaps' at the corners.

Corners

1. Fold the corners or flaps and finger press down the corner well. The seam will be visible and followed for sewing. Mark the seam if you prefer. Sew a mitered corner by inserting the needle at the side seam's 1/4" mark. Trim corner to a 1/4" seam and press the seam open. Clip fabric close to the seam where it meets at the corner. This will help it to lay flat.

2. Turn inside out and press well. Use a decorative stitch to topstitch around the seam line of the napkin.

3. To add JOY appliqué, trace letters from the template below onto fusible web. Refer to General Instructions – Appliqué on pages 8-9. Dot the wrong side of letters on all edges with Liquid Stitch®. Place on napkins and finger press. Let dry. Press with iron. If using glue there will be no need to appliqué with thread.

JOY Templates
Cut 1 of each letter

Acknowledgements

I wish to extend my heartfelt thanks -

To my Husband, Bart: who encourages me to fly. Your ability to enable my passion for quilting over the years has been such a gift. Thank you for sharing your quick wit and humor, for putting up with the mounds of fabric all over the house, and especially for going with the flow while I forgo making dinner as I work to meet a deadline. White marks in heaven for you! OXOX

To my sister, Heidi: Thank you for the long distance cheerleading, love, support and consulting with me as I worked on this book. We have had a remarkable journey together in this business and I can't imagine not having you by my side to share it with. You encourage me to do my best and love what I do. Our bond as sisters is such a comfort to me. Love you!

To my daughter, Megan: Sharing & creating with you was always a dream that I had envisioned for us as you grew into adulthood. Your talents inspire me and I am thankful that we can work together in a business that we both love and thrive in. Thank you for your love and support. I ♥ you.

To my dear friend, Linda: Your time, talent & encouragement keeps me grounded and focused. Thank you for jumping in to lend a hand, listening when I need to solve a problem and sharing your huge heart. I am grateful for our enduring friendship.

And a special thank you to the staff at Landauer Publishing who have assisted me in so many ways to bring this book to fruition. I appreciate the opportunity you have given me to create in my own way. You are all amazing women and you have my sincere gratitude. It has been a pleasure to work with you. Jeramy, thank you for believing in me.

Credits

A special thank you to my friends at Robert Kaufman Fabrics & Michael Miller Fabrics; they have provided many of the incredible collections of fabrics used in projects for this book. You are an invaluable resource to me and are so greatly appreciated.

Quilting

My sincere appreciation to the talented quilters whose artistic interpretation added so much to the projects in the book -

Lemon & Cherry Collections   **Heidi Fisher, my talented and fabulous sister!**

Orange and Pear Collections   **Lynn Witzenburg**

Quilts and projects

Design, piecing, and stitching   **Dodi Poulsen**